Heinemann Professional Publishing Ltd
Halley Court, Jordan Hill, Oxford OX2 8EJ

OXFORD LONDON MELBOURNE AUCKLAND

First published 1984
Reprinted 1984, 1985, 1986, 1987, 1988

© Malcolm H. B. McDonald 1984

ISBN 0 434 91230 1

Photoset by Rowlands Phototypesetting Ltd
Printed in Great Britain by
LR Printing Services Ltd,
Crawley, Sussex

Marketing Plans

How to Prepare Them
How to Use Them

Malcolm H. B. McDonald
MA(Oxon), MSc, PhD, FInstM

*Published on behalf of the Institute of Marketing
and the CAM Foundation*

Heinemann Professional Publishing

Marketing Plans

The Institute of Marketing

Marketing means Business

The Institute of Marketing was founded in 1911.
It is now the largest and most successful marketing
management organisation in Europe with over
20,000 members and 16,000 students throughout
the world. The Institute is a democratic
organisation and is run for the members by the
members with the assistance of a permanent staff
headed by the Director General. The
Headquarters of the Institute are at Moor Hall,
Cookham, near Maidenhead, in Berkshire.

Objectives: The objectives of the Institute are to
develop knowledge about marketing, to provide
services for members and registered students and
to make the principles and practices of marketing
more widely known and used throughout industry
and commerce.

Range of activities: The Institute's activities are
divided into four main areas:
  Membership and membership activities
  Corporate activities
  Marketing education
  Marketing training

OTHER TITLES IN THE SERIES

The Marketing Book
Michael J. Baker (ed.)

Marketing Communications
C. J. Coulson-Thomas

Marketing Research for Managers
S. Crouch

Case Studies in International Marketing
P. Doyle and N. A. Hart

The Principles and Practice of Selling
A. Gillam

Essentials of Statistics in Marketing
C. S. Greensted, A. K. S. Jardine, and J. D. Macfarlane

A Career in Marketing, Advertising and Public Relations
N. A. Hart and G. W. Lamb

The Practice of Advertising
N. A. Hart and J. O'Connor

Glossary of Marketing Terms
N. A. Hart and J. Stapleton

The Practice of Public Relations
W. Howard

Legal Aspects of Marketing
J. L. Livermore

A Modern Approach to Economics
F. Livesey

How to Sell a Service
Malcolm H. B. McDonald

Case Studies in Marketing, Advertising and Public Relations
C. McIver

Business Analysis for Marketing Managers
L. A. Rogers

Profitable Product Management
J. Ward

Behavioural Aspects of Marketing
K. Williams

Business Organization
R. J. Williamson

Management Controls and Marketing Planning
R. M. S. Wilson

The Fundamentals and Practice of Marketing
J. Wilmshurst

Bargaining for Results
J. Winkler

Pricing for Results
J. Winkler

Contents

Preface

The purpose of this book is quite simply to explain and demonstrate how to prepare and use a marketing plan.

It is based on our research into the marketing planning practices of industrial companies, which has revealed marketing planning as an area of major weakness. Almost without exception, companies that thought they were planning were in fact only forecasting and budgeting, and suffered grave operational difficulties as a result. The problem is not that the *philosophy* of marketing is not believed; rather it is that most companies, particularly industrial goods companies, just cannot make it work.

This is largely because of ignorance about the process of planning their marketing activities, for which little help is provided in the extant body of literature. Books or articles often turn out to be about the management of the several elements of the marketing mix rather than about how the process of combining them into a coherent plan can be managed. Others treat marketing planning in such a generalized way that it is difficult to distil from them any guidance of operational significance. Finally there are many excellent papers about individual aspects of the marketing planning process.

The truth is, of course, that the actual *process* of marketing planning is simple in outline. Any book will tell us that it consists of: a situation review; assumptions; objectives; strategies; programmes; and measurement and review. What other books *do not* tell us is that there are a number of contextual issues that have to be considered that make marketing planning one of the most baffling of all management problems.

Here are some of those issues:

When should it be done, *how often*, by *whom*, and *how*?
Is it different in a *large* and a *small* company?
Is it different in a *diversified* and an *undiversified* company?
Is it different in an *international* and a *domestic* company?

What is the role of the *chief executive*?
What is the role of the *planning department*?
Should marketing planning be *top-down* or *bottom-up*?
What is the relationship between *operational* (one year) and *strategic* (longer term) planning?

Since effective marketing planning lies at the heart of a company's revenue-earning activities, it is not surprising that there is a great demand for a guide which strips away the confusion and mystery surrounding this subject and helps firms to get to grips with it in a practical and down-to-earth manner.

This book explains what marketing is, how the marketing planning process works, how to carry out a marketing audit, how to set marketing objectives and strategies, how to schedule and cost out what has to be done to achieve the objectives, and how to design and implement a simple marketing planning system.

We believe our approach is both logical and practical. The text is an integral part of the resource *Marketing Plans: how to prepare them, how to use them* and is designed to be used in conjunction with material from other parts of the resource. This includes workbooks designed to enable managers to practise the skills and techniques explained in the text, a comprehensive tutor's guide, tape/slide presentations, and a collection of case studies and exercises.

The present book*, however, has been designed to be self-sufficient in explaining and demonstrating the key areas of marketing planning. Thus, while the individual reader of this text would benefit from the total resource, he will find no unexplained gaps or cross-references in this text.

Malcolm H. B. McDonald
Cranfield School of Management
January 1984

---

*Further details of the PhD research on which this book is based are available from Dr Malcolm H. B. McDonald, Director of the Cranfield Marketing Planning Centre, Cranfield School of Management, Cranfield, Bedford, England, MK43 0AL.

1 Understanding the Marketing Process

The marketing concept

In 1776, when Adam Smith said that consumption is the sole end and purpose of production, he was in fact describing what in recent years has become known as the *marketing concept*. Basically, the central idea of marketing is of a matching between a company's capabilities and the wants of customers in order to achieve the goals of the firm.

It is important at this stage to understand the difference between the marketing concept (often referred to as 'market orientation') and the *marketing mix*. This latter term describes the various tools and techniques used by marketing people in order to implement the marketing concept.

For the sake of simplicity, these are often written about and referred to as the four Ps, these being Product, Price, Place and Promotion.

However, before any meaningful discussion can take place about how the marketing function should be managed, it is vital to have a full understanding about the idea of marketing itself (the marketing concept), and it is this issue that we principally address in this chapter.

Company capabilities

We have said that marketing is a matching process between a company's capabilities and the wants of customers. In Chapter 4 we will explain what we mean when we talk about customer wants. But for now, it is important to understand what we mean when we talk about a company's capabilities. To explain this more fully, let us imagine that we have been made redundant and have decided to set ourselves up in our own business.

1

The first thing we would have to do is to decide what it is that we can actually *do*. In answering this question we would quickly realize that our actual knowledge and skills restrict us very severely to certain obvious areas. For example, it would be difficult for a former sales manager to set himself up in business as an estate agent, or for an estate agent to start a marketing consultancy, unless, of course, both had the necessary skills and knowledge. A little thought will confirm that it is exactly the same for a company. Many commercial disasters have resulted from companies diversifying into activities for which they were basically unsuited.

One such case concerns a firm making connectors for the military and aviation markets. When these traditional markets went into decline, the company diversified into making connectors for several industrial markets such as consumer durables, automobiles and so on. Unfortunately these markets were so completely different from the ones that the company had been used to that they quickly went into a loss-making situation. Whereas the connector which the company had previously manufactured had been a highly engineered product made to the specifications of a few high technology customers, the company now had to mass produce simple connectors for broad markets. This meant making for stock and carrying field inventory. It also meant low competitive prices. The sales force did not know how to cope with the demands of their new markets. They had been used to making one or two calls a day and to having detailed technical discussions with buyers, whereas now they were expected to make eight or nine calls a day and to sell against many competitive products. Furthermore, the company just did not have the right image to succeed in the market. The results of all this were very serious indeed.

The lesson simply is that all firms have a unique set of capabilities in the form of resources and management skills which are not necessarily capable of taking advantage of *all* market opportunities as effectively, hence as competitively, as other firms. To summarize, the matching process between a company's capabilities and customer wants is fundamental to commercial success. That this is so will become clearer as we get further into the task of explaining the role and the nature of marketing.

The marketing environment

This matching process takes place in what we can call the *marketing environment*, which is the milieu in which the firm is operating. Perhaps the most obvious constituent of the marketing environment is our competitors, for what they do vitally affects our own behaviour as a company.

The point is that, since what our competitors do so vitally affects our own decisions, it is necessary to find some way of monitoring this and other elements of the environment and of building this into our decision-making process. In Chapter 11 we show how this can be done.

The *political, fiscal, economic* and *legal* policies of the governments of the countries where we sell our goods also determine what we can do. For example, inflation reduces the discretionary spending power of consumers, and this can result in market decline. Legislation concerning such things as labelling, packaging, advertising, environmentalism, and so on, all affect the way we run our business, and all these things have to be taken account of when we make our plans.

Technology is constantly changing, and we can no longer assume that our current range of products will continue to be demanded by our customers. For example, the introduction of non-drip paint had a profound effect on what had traditionally been a stable market. People discovered that they could use paint without causing a mess, and eventually this product was demanded in new kinds of outlets such as supermarkets. One can imagine what happened to some of those paint manufacturers who continued to make only their traditional products and to distribute them only through the more traditional outlets.

Such a change would also call for a change in pricing, promotional and distribution policies, and failure to realize this and to act accordingly would probably result in commercial failure.

The point is that the environment in which we operate is not controlled by us, and it is dynamic. Hence it must be constantly monitored.

So far we have talked about the three constituent parts of what we have described as a matching process:

> the capabilities of a firm
> the wants of customers
> the marketing environment

Diagrammatically, it is shown in Figure 1.1.

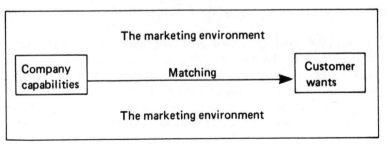

Figure 1.1

Customer wants

Although we shall be dealing with this subject in Chapter 4, let us briefly turn our attention to the subject of customer wants, so that we can complete our understanding of what marketing is.

Perhaps one of the greatest areas for misunderstanding in marketing concerns this question of customer wants. Companies are accused of manipulating innocent consumers by making them want things they do not really need.

If this were so, we would not have a situation in which about 80 per cent of all new products launched actually fail! The fact is people have always had needs, such as, say, for home entertainment. What changes in the course of time is the way people satisfy this need. For example, television was only commercially viable because people needed home entertainment, and this was yet another way of fulfilling that need.

But let us not be fooled into believing that the customer in the end does not have the final say. All customer needs have many different ways of being satisfied, and wherever people have *choice* they will choose that product which they perceive as offering the greatest benefits to them at whatever price they are prepared to pay.

What this means in effect, since all companies incur costs in taking goods or services to the market, is that *profit* is the only measure of efficacy or worth of what the firm is doing. Cheapness or efficiency, or any other measure for that matter, are not criteria of effectiveness, since there is little point in producing, say, small, cheap, efficient black and white television sets if what people want are small, cheap, efficient colour television sets.

Let us explain why this should be so in all commercial operations.

Since costs are incurred in producing goods, it is necessary to find customers to buy those goods at a sufficiently high price and in sufficient volume (margin × turnover) to enable the company to cover its costs and to make a surplus (or profit). This is an economic necessity to enable the company to stay in business, and means that unless what you are making is seen by customers as satisfying their wants, they will not buy your product.

Thus, if you make small, cheap, efficient black and white television sets, and there is a long-term fundamental decline in demand for such items, unless you are prepared to change so as to be more in time with what the market wants, in the end you will go out of business. Even less sensible would be for a government, or a parent company, to subsidize such an operation, since we know that to go on producing what people do not want is economically inefficient, especially when people will get what they want from abroad if they cannot buy it here.

The same line of reasoning must also apply to those who continually counsel increased productivity as the answer to our economic problems. Unfortunately any additional production would more than likely end up in stock unless people actually wanted what was being produced.

It would be different, of course, if there was only a temporary hiccup in demand, but unfortunately this is rarely the case, because markets are dynamic and we must learn as a company to adapt and change as our markets mutate.

Central to this question of customer wants is an understanding that there is rarely such a thing as 'a market'. In reality, most markets consist of a number of sub-markets, each of which is different. For example, the airline market consists of freight and passenger transport. The passenger side can be subdivided further into VFR (visiting friends and relatives), high rated (business travel), charter, and so on. Failure to understand the needs of these very different customer groups would result in failure to provide the desired services at an acceptable price.

Of course, it is not quite as easy as this, which is why we devote the whole of Chapter 4 to this very important aspect of what we call 'market segmentation management'. But for now all that it is necessary to understand is that our ability to identify groups of customer wants which our particular company capabilities are able to satisfy profitably is central to marketing management.

The marketing mix

As we have already said, the marketing mix is a term used to describe the tools and techniques of marketing. Thus, in order for the matching process to take place we need *information*. External and internal marketing information flows (marketing research) are discussed further in Chapter 11.

Having found out what customers want, we must develop products to satisfy those wants. This is known as 'product management' and is discussed in Chapter 5. Obviously we must charge a price for our products, and this is discussed in Chapter 9.

We must also get our products into our customers' hands, thus giving a time and a place utility to our product. Distribution is discussed in Chapter 10.

All that remains now is to tell our customers about our products, for we can be certain that customers will not beat a path to our door to buy whatever it is we are making. Here we must consider all forms of communication, especially advertising, personal selling, and sales promotion. These are discussed in Chapters 7 and 8.

Finally we must consider how to tie it all together in the form of a marketing plan. This latter point is so important that the whole of the next two chapters are devoted to a discussion of the marketing planning process.

What is the difference between marketing and selling?

It should by now be obvious that those people who talk about 'the sharp end', by which they usually mean personal selling, as being the only thing that matters in marketing, have probably got it wrong.

Selling is just one aspect of communication with customers, and to say that it is the only thing that matters is to ignore the importance of product management, pricing, distribution and other forms of communication in achieving profitable sales. Selling is just one part of this process, in which the transaction is actually clinched. It is the culmination of the marketing process, and success will only be possible if all the other elements of the marketing mix have been properly managed. In other words, the more attention that is paid to finding out what customers want, to developing products to satisfy these wants, to pricing at a level consistent with the benefits offered, to gaining distribution, and to communicating effectively with our target market, the more likely we are to be able to exchange contracts through the personal selling process.

Likewise it is naive to assume that marketing is all about advertising, since it is by now clear that advertising is only one aspect of communication.

Many firms waste their advertising expenditure because they have not properly identified what their target market is. For example one public transport company spent a quarter of a million pounds advertising how reliable their bus service was when in reality utilization of buses by the public was declining because they somehow felt that buses were working class! This was a classic case of believing that advertising will increase sales irrespective of what you say. Had this company done its research, it could have decided to what extent and how advertising could be used to overcome this prejudice. As it was, the company spent a small fortune telling people something that was largely irrelevant!

In reality many companies spend more on advertising when times are good and less on advertising when times are bad. Cutting the advertising budget is often seen as an easy way of boosting the profit and loss account when a firm is below its budgeted level of profit, and this tendency is encouraged by the fact that this can be done without any apparent immediate adverse effect on sales. Unfortunately, this is just another classic piece of misunderstanding about marketing and about the role of advertising in particular. It is naive in the extreme to assume that advertising effectiveness can be measured in terms of sales when it is only a part of the total marketing process.

Are industrial and consumer marketing different?

The central ideas of marketing are universal and it makes no difference whether we are marketing furnaces or margarine. The problems arise when we try to implement marketing ideas in industrial goods companies.

Industrial goods are simply those goods sold to industrial businesses, institutional or government buyers for incorporation into their own products, to be resold, or to be used by them within their own business. Principal types of industrial goods are raw materials, components, capital goods and maintenance, repair and operating goods and equipment.

The fact that the share of world trade enjoyed by some industrial countries has slumped so dramatically over the past thirty years is not generally because their products were not as good as those produced by other countries, but because they failed to *market* them as effectively as their competitors, and there is much government, university and trade body evidence to support this view.

One reason for this is that many industrial goods companies naively believe that the name of the game is making well-engineered products. Making well-engineered products is all some companies are concerned about, in spite of the fact that all the evidence points to the conclusion that more often than not it is for other reasons that the final choice is actually made. Failure to understand the importance of market segmentation (to be discussed in Chapter 4), market share, service, and reputation, among other things, is the principal reason why such companies fail to compete successfully in so many world markets. Making what they consider to be good products and then giving them to the sales force to get rid of is just not enough.

But quite apart from the fact that there appears to be a sort of status about being in engineering which acts as a barrier to the consideration of marketing issues, it is also a fact that marketing is difficult in many industrial markets. This makes it inevitable that managers will resort to doing things they can understand. For example, demand for all industrial products is derived from the demand for consumer products, which adds greater uncertainty to decision-making and makes forecasting extremely difficult.

It can be readily appreciated from Figure 1.2 that the further a company gets from the eventual consumer, the less control it has over demand. Take

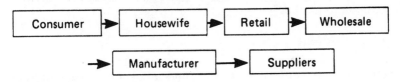

Figure 1.2

the example of a brewer. He can communicate direct with his consumers whereas the company making his plant, and the suppliers in turn to the plant company, are in the final analysis dependent on the ultimate consumer, and they cannot influence what he does.

Also, information about industrial markets is not so readily available as in consumer goods markets, which makes it more difficult to measure changes in market share. And there are other difficulties besides these which make marketing in the industrial area more difficult.

Unfortunately, the answer to this problem by many companies has been to recruit a 'marketing man' and leave him to get on with the job of marketing. But it will now be obvious that such a solution can never work, because the marketing concept, if it is to work at all, has to be understood and practised by all executives in a firm, not just by the marketing manager. Otherwise everyone goes on behaving just as they did before and the marketing man quickly becomes ineffective.

Do you need a marketing department?

This brings us finally to the question about whether it is necessary for a company to have a marketing department.

It is not essential to have a formalized marketing department for the analysis, planning and control of the matching process. This is particularly so in small, undiversified companies where the chief executive has an in-depth understanding of his customers' needs. Even in large companies it is not necessary to have a marketing department, because the management of products can be left to the engineers, pricing can be managed by the accountants, distribution can be managed by distribution specialists, and selling and advertising can be managed by the Sales Manager. However, as a company's product range and customer types grow, so it usually becomes necessary to organize the management of marketing under one central control function, otherwise there is a danger of ending up with the kind of product which is brilliant technically but disastrous commercially.

Much more important, however, than who is responsible for marketing in an organization, is the question of its marketing orientation, i.e. the degree to which the company as a whole understands the importance of finding out what customer groups want and of organizing all the company's resources to satisfy those wants at a profit.

Application questions

1 Describe as best you can what you think marketing means in your company.

2   Describe the role of your marketing department, if you have one.
3   If you do not have a marketing department, describe how decisions are
    made in respect of the following:

> the product itself
> price
> customer service levels
> physical distribution
> advertising
> sales promotion
> the sales force
> information about markets

4   How do you distinguish between marketing and selling in your org-
    anization?
5   Would you say your products are what the market wants, or what you
    prefer to produce?
6   Do you start your planning process with a sales forecast, and then work
    out a budget, or do you start by setting marketing objectives, which are
    based on a thorough review of the previous year's performance? If the
    former, describe why you think this is better than the latter.

2 The Marketing Planning Process: 1
The Main Steps

Any manager will readily agree that a sensible way to manage the sales and marketing function is to find a systematic way of identifying a range of options, to choose one or more of them, then to schedule and cost out what has to be done to achieve the objectives. This process can be defined as *marketing planning*, which is the planned application of marketing resources to achieve marketing objectives.

The problem is, that while as a process it is intellectually simple to understand, in practice it is the most difficult of all marketing tasks. The reason is that it involves bringing together into one coherent plan all the elements of marketing, and in order to do this at least some degree of institutionalized procedures is necessary. It is this which seems to cause so much difficulty for companies.

The purpose of this chapter is to explain as simply as possible what marketing planning is and how the process works before going on to expand on the more important components of marketing planning in later chapters.

One reason for this difficulty is that there is not much guidance available to management on how the process itself might be managed, proceeding as it does from reviews to objectives, strategies, programmes, budgets and back again, until some kind of acceptable compromise is reached between what is desirable and what is practicable, given all the constraints that any company has.

Another reason is that a planning system itself is little more than a structured approach to the process just described. But because of the varying size, complexity, character and diversity of commercial operations, there can be no such thing as an 'off the peg' system that can be implemented without some pretty fundamental amendments to suit the situation-specific requirements of each company.

Also, the degree to which any company can develop an integrated, coordinated and consistent plan depends on a deep understanding of the marketing planning process itself as a means of sharpening the focus within all levels of management within an organization.

Why is marketing planning essential?

There can be little doubt that marketing planning is essential when we consider the increasingly hostile and complex environment in which companies operate. Hundreds of external and internal factors interact in a bafflingly complex way to affect our ability to achieve profitable sales. Also, let us consider for a moment the four typical objectives which companies set: maximizing revenue; maximizing profits; maximizing return on investment; and minimizing costs. Each one of these has its own special appeal to different managers within the company, depending on the nature of their particular function. In reality the best that can ever be achieved is a kind of 'optimum compromise', because each of these objectives could be considered to be in conflict in terms of equivalences.

Managers of a company have to have some understanding or view about how all these variables interact and managers try to be rational about their business decisions, no matter how important intuition, feel and experience are as contributory factors in this process of rationality.

Most managers accept that some kind of formalized procedure for marketing planning helps sharpen this rationality so as to reduce the complexity of business operations and add a dimension of realism to the company's hopes for the future. Because it is so difficult, however, most companies rely only on sales forecasting and budgeting systems. It is a well-known fact that any fool can write figures down! All too frequently, however, they bear little relationship to the real opportunities and problems facing a company. It is far more difficult to write down marketing objectives and strategies.

The marketing planning process

Figure 2.1 illustrates the several stages that have to be gone through in order to arrive at a marketing plan.

A recent study of leading companies carried out by Cranfield showed that a marketing plan should contain:

A summary of all the principal external factors which affected the company's marketing performance during the previous year, together with a statement of the company's strengths and weaknesses *vis-à-vis*

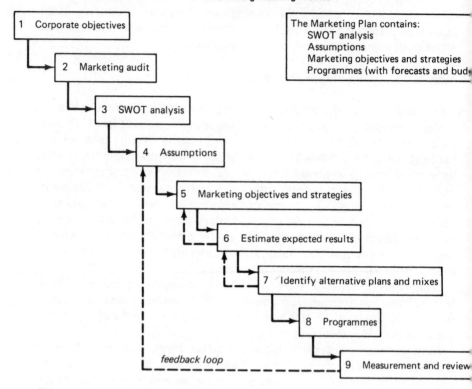

Figure 2.1

the competition. This is what we call a SWOT (i.e. strengths, weaknesses, opportunities, threats) analysis.

Some assumptions about the key determinants of marketing success and failure.

Overall marketing objectives and strategies.

Programmes containing details of timing, responsibilities and costs, with sales forecasts and budgets.

Each of the stages illustrated here will be discussed in more detail later in this chapter.

The dotted lines joining up steps 5, 6 and 7 are meant to indicate the reality of the planning process, in that it is likely that each of these steps will have to be gone through more than once before final programmes can be written.

Although research has shown these marketing planning steps to be universally applicable, the degree to which each of the separate steps in the diagram needs to be formalized depends to a large extent on the size and nature of the company. For example an *undiversified* company generally uses less formalized procedures, since top management tends to have greater functional knowledge and expertise than subordinates and because the lack of diversity of operations enables direct control to be exercised over most of the key determinants of success. Thus, situation reviews, the setting of marketing objectives, and so on, are not always made explicit in writing, although these steps still have to be gone through.

In contrast, in a *diversified* company, it is usually not possible for top management to have greater functional knowledge and expertise than subordinate management, hence the whole planning process tends to be more formalized in order to provide a consistent discipline for those who have to make the decisions throughout the organization.

Either way, however, there is now a substantial body of evidence to show that formalized marketing planning procedures generally result in greater profitability and stability in the long term and also help to reduce friction and operational difficulties within organizations.

Where marketing planning has failed, it has generally been because companies have placed too much emphasis on the procedures themselves and the resulting paperwork, rather than on generating information useful to and consumable by management. Also, where companies relegate marketing planning to someone called a 'planner', it invariably fails, for the single reason that planning for line management cannot be delegated to a third party. The real role of the 'planner' should be to help those responsible for implementation to plan. Failure to recognize this simple fact can be disastrous. Finally, planning failures often result from companies trying too much, too quickly, and without training staff in the use of procedures.

One Swedish company selling batteries internationally tried unsuccessfully three times to introduce a marketing planning system, each one failing because management throughout the organization were confused by what was being asked of them. Also, not only did they not understand the need for the new systems, but they were not provided with the necessary resources to make the system work effectively. Training of managers, and careful thought about resource requirements, would have largely overcome this company's planning problems.

In contrast, a major multinational oil company, having suffered grave profitability and operational difficulties through not having an effective marketing planning system, introduced one over a three-year period that included a training programme in the use of the new procedures and the provision of adequate resources to make them work effectively. This company is now firmly in control of its diverse activities and has regained its confidence and its profitability.

We can now look at the marketing planning process in more detail, starting with a look at the marketing audit. So far we have looked at the need for marketing planning and outlined a series of steps that have to be gone through in order to arrive at a marketing plan. However, any plan will only be as good as the information on which it is based, and the marketing audit is the means by which information for planning is organized.

What is a marketing audit?

Auditing as a process is usually associated with the financial side of a business and is conducted according to a defined set of accounting standards, which are well documented, easily understood, and which therefore lend themselves readily to the auditing process. The total business process, although more complicated, innovative and relying more on judgement than on a set of rules, is still nevertheless capable of being audited.

Basically, an audit is the means by which a company can understand how it relates to the environment in which it operates. It is the means by which a company can identify its own strengths and weaknesses as they relate to external opportunities and threats. It is thus a way of helping management to select a position in that environment based on known factors.

Expressed in its simplest form, if the purpose of a corporate plan is to answer three central questions:

Where is the company now?
Where does the company want to go?
How should the company organize its resources to get there?

then the audit is the means by which the first of these questions is answered. An audit is a systematic, critical and unbiased review and appraisal of the environment and of the company's operations. A marketing audit is part of the larger management audit and is concerned with the marketing environment and marketing operations.

Why is there a need for an audit?

Often the need for an audit does not manifest itself until things start to go wrong for a company, such as declining sales, falling margins, lost market share, underutilized production capacity, and so on.

At times like these, management often attempts to treat the wrong symptoms. For example, introducing new products or dropping products, reorganizing the sales force, reducing prices, and cutting costs, are just some of the actions which could be taken. But such measures are unlikely to be effective if there are more fundamental problems which have not been identified. Of course, if the company could survive long enough, it might eventually solve its problems through a process of elimination! Essentially, the argument is that problems have to be properly defined, and the audit is a means of helping to define them.

To summarize, the audit is a structured approach to the collection and analysis of information and data in the complex business environment and an essential prerequisite to problem-solving.

The form of the audit

Any company carrying out an audit will be faced with two kinds of variables. Firstly, there are variables over which the company has no direct control. These usually take the form of what can be described as environmental and market variables. Secondly, there are variables over which the company has complete control. These we can call operational variables.

This gives us a clue as to how we can structure an audit. That is to say, in two parts:

External audit
Internal audit

The *external audit* is concerned with the uncontrollable variables, whilst the *internal audit* is concerned with the controllable variables.

The external audit starts with an examination of information on the general economy and then moves on to the outlook for the health and growth of the markets served by the company.

The purpose of the internal audit is to assess the organization's resources as they relate to the environment and *vis-à-vis* the resources of competitors.

The place of the marketing audit in the management unit

The term *management audit* (Figure 2.2) merely means a company-wide audit which includes an assessment of all internal resources against the external environment. In practice, the best way to carry out a management audit is to conduct a separate audit of each major management function. Thus the marketing audit is merely part of the larger management audit, in the same way that the production audit is.

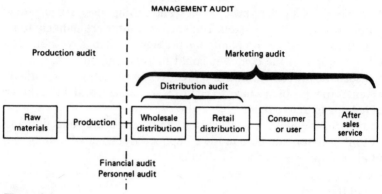

Figure 2.2

Here is a checklist of areas which should be investigated as part of the marketing audit. This is shown in greater detail in Table 2.1.

Internal audit

Marketing operational variables
Own company
Sales (total, by geographical location, by industrial type, by customer, by product)
Market shares
Profit margins/costs
Marketing procedures
Marketing organization
Marketing information/research
Marketing mix variables as follows:
    Product management
    Price
    Distribution
    Promotion

External audit

Business and economic environment
Economic
Political/fiscal/legal
Social/cultural
Technological
Intra-company

The market
Total market, size, growth and trends (value/volume)
Market characteristics, developments and trends
    Products
    Prices
    Physical distribution
    Channels
    Customers/consumers
    Communication
    Industry practices

Competition
Major competitors
Size
Market shares/coverage
Market standing/reputation
Production capabilities
Distribution policies
Marketing methods
Extent of diversification
Personnel issues
International links
Profitability
Key strengths and weaknesses

Table 2.1   Marketing audit checklist
(fuller details)

INTERNAL (Strengths and Weaknesses)
Own company
Sales (total, by geographical location, by industrial type, by customer, by product)
Market shares
Profit margins
Marketing procedures
Marketing organization
Sales/marketing control data
Marketing mix variables as follows:

Market research	Samples
Product development	Exhibitions
Product range	Selling
Product quality	Sales aids
Unit of sale	Point of sale
Stock levels	Advertising
Distribution	Sales promotion
Dealer support	Public relations
Pricing, discounts, credit	After sales service
Packaging	Training

Operations and resources
Marketing objectives
Are the marketing objectives clearly stated and consistent with marketing and corporate objectives?
Marketing strategy
What is the strategy for achieving the stated objectives? Are sufficient resources available to achieve these objectives? Are the available resources sufficient and optimally allocated across elements of the marketing mix?
Structure
Are the marketing responsibilities and authorities clearly structured along functional, product, end-user, and territorial lines?
Information system
Is the marketing intelligence system producing accurate, sufficient and timely information about developments in the market place?
Is information gathered being used effectively in making marketing decisions?
Planning system
Is the marketing planning system well conceived and effective?
Control system
Do control mechanisms and procedures exist within the group to ensure planned objectives are achieved, e.g. meeting overall objectives, etc.?
Functional efficiency
Are internal communications within the group effective?
Interfunctional efficiency
Are there any problems between marketing and other corporate functions?
Is the question of centralized versus decentralized marketing an issue in the company?

Table 2.1. – *cont.*

Profitability analysis
Is the profitability performance monitored by product, served markets, etc., to assess where the best profits and biggest costs of the operation are located?
Cost-effectiveness analysis
Do any current marketing actitivies seem to have excess costs?
Are these valid or could they be reduced?

EXTERNAL (Opportunities and Threats)
Business and economic environment

Economic	Inflation, unemployment, energy, price, volatility, materials availability, etc.	as they affect your business
Political/fiscal/legal	Nationalization, union legislation, taxation, duty increases, regulatory constraints (e.g. labelling, product quality, packaging, trade practices, advertising, pricing, etc.)	as they affect your business
Social/cultural	Education, immigration, emigration, religion, environment, population distribution and dynamics (e.g. age distribution, regional distribution, etc.), changes in consumer life style, etc.	as they affect your business
Technological	Aspects of product and/or production technology which could profoundly affect the economics of the industry (e.g. new technology, cost savings, materials, components, equipment, machinery, methods and systems, availability of substitutes, etc.)	as they affect your business
Intracompany	Capital investment, closures, strikes, etc.	as they affect your business

The market

Total market	Size, growth, and trends (value, volume).
Market characteristics	Developments and trends.
	Products: principal products bought; end-use of products; product characteristics (weights, measures, sizes, physical characteristics, packaging, accessories, associated products, etc.).
	Prices: price levels and range; terms and conditions of sale; normal trade practices; official regulations, etc.
	Physical distribution: principal method of physical distribution.

Table 2.1. – *cont.*

	Channels: principal channels; purchasing patterns (e.g. types of product bought, prices paid, etc.); purchasing ability; geographical location; stocks; turnover; profits; needs; tastes; attitudes; decision-makers, bases of purchasing decision; etc. *Communication:* principal methods of communication, e.g. sales force, advertising, direct response, exhibitions, public relations, etc. *Industry practices:* e.g. trade associations, government bodies, historical attitudes, interfirm comparisons; etc.
Competition	*Industry structure:* make-up of companies in the industry, major market standing/reputation; extent of excess capacity; production capability; distribution capability; marketing methods; competitive arrangements; extent of diversification into other areas by major companies in the industry; new entrants; mergers; acquisitions; bankruptcies; significant aspects; international links; key strengths and weaknesses. *Industry profitability:* financial and non-financial barriers to entry; industry profitability and the relative performance of individual companies; structure of operating costs; investment; effect on return on investment of changes in price; volume; cost of investment; source of industry profits; etc.

Each one of these headings should be examined with a view to isolating those factors that are considered critical to the company's performance. Initially, the auditor's task is to screen the enormous amount of information and data for validity and relevance. Some data and information will have to be reorganized into a more easily usable form, and judgement will have to be applied to decide what further data and information are necessary to a proper definition of the problem.

Behind the summary, there are fuller details of all the questions that should be asked as part of the audit.

Thus there are basically two phases which comprise the auditing process:
1 Identification, measurement, collection, and analysis of all the relevant facts and opinions which impinge on a company's problems.
2 The application of judgement to uncertain areas which are remaining following this analysis.

When should the marketing audit be carried out?

A mistaken belief held by many people is that the marketing audit should be a last-ditch, end-of-the-road attempt to define a company's marketing problem, or at best something done by an independent body from time to time to ensure that a company is on the right lines. However, since marketing is such a complex function, it seems illogical not to carry out a pretty thorough situation analysis at least once a year at the beginning of the planning cycle.

There is much evidence to show that many highly successful companies, as well as using normal information and control procedures and marketing research throughout the year, also start their planning cycle each year with a formal review, through an audit-type process, of everything that has had an important influence on marketing activities. Certainly in many leading consumer goods companies, the annual self-audit approach is a tried and tested discipline integrated into the management process.

Who should carry out the audit?

Occasionally it may be justified to hire outside consultants to carry out a marketing audit to check that a company is getting the most out of its resources. However, it seems an unnecessary expense to have this done every year. The answer, therefore, is to have an audit carried out annually by the company's own line managers on their own areas of responsibility.

Objections to this usually centre around the problems of time and objectivity. In practice, these problems are overcome by institutionalizing procedures in as much detail as possible so that all managers have to conform to a disciplined approach, and secondly by thorough training in the use of the procedures themselves. However, even this will not result in achieving the purpose of an audit unless a rigorous discipline is applied from the highest down to the lowest levels of management involved in the audit. Such a discipline is usually successful in helping managers to avoid the sort of tunnel vision that often results from a lack of critical appraisal.

What happens to the results of the audit?

The only remaining question is what happens to the results of the audit? Some companies consume valuable resources carrying out audits that bring very little by way of actionable results.

Indeed, there is always the danger that at the audit stage insufficient attention is paid to the need to concentrate on analysis that determines which trends and developments will actually affect the company. Whilst the checklist demonstrates the completeness of logic and analysis, the people carrying out the audit should discipline themselves to omit from their plans all the information that is not central to the company's marketing problems. Thus, inclusion of research reports, or overdetailed sales performance histories by product which lead to no logical actions whatever, only serve to rob the audit of focus and reduce its relevance.

Since the objective of the audit is to indicate what a company's marketing objectives and strategies should be, it follows that it would be helpful if some format could be found for organizing the major findings. One useful way of doing this is in the form of a SWOT analysis. This is a summary of the audit under the headings, internal strengths and weaknesses as they relate to external opportunities and threats.

This SWOT analysis should, if possible, contain not more than four or five pages of commentary focusing on *key* factors only. It should highlight internal *differential* strengths and weaknesses *vis-à-vis* competitors and *key* external opportunities and threats. A summary of reasons for good or bad performance should be included. It should be interesting to read, contain concise statements, include only relevant and important data, and give greater emphasis to creative analysis.

To summarize, carrying out a regular and thorough marketing audit in a structured manner will go a long way towards giving a company a knowledge of the business, trends in the market, and where value is added by competitors, as the basis for setting objectives and strategies.

How marketing planning relates to corporate planning

Before turning our attention to the other important steps in the marketing planning process, it would be useful to discuss how marketing planning relates to the corporate planning process.

There are five steps in the corporate planning process. As can be seen from Table 2.2, the starting point is usually a statement of corporate financial objectives for the long-range planning period of the company, which are often expressed in terms of turnover, profit before tax, and return on investment.

More often than not, this long-range planning horizon is five years, but the precise period should be determined by the nature of the markets in which the company operates. For example, five years would not be a long enough period for a glass manufacturer, since it takes that period of time to commission a new furnace, whereas in some fashion industries, five years would be too long. A useful guideline in determining the planning horizon is that there should be a market for the company products for long enough at least to amortize any capital investment associated with those products.

The next step is the *management audit*, which we have already discussed. This is an obvious activity to follow on with, since a thorough situation review, particularly in the area of marketing, should enable the company to determine whether it will be able to meet the long-range financial targets

Table 2.2 Marketing planning and its place in the corporate planning cycle

Step 1	2 Management audit	3 Objective and strategy setting	4 Plans	5 Corporate plans
Corporate financial objectives	*Marketing audit* Marketing	Marketing objectives, strategies	Marketing plan	Issue of corporate plan, to include corporate objectives and strategies; production objectives and strategies, etc.; long-range profit and loss accounts; balance sheets
	Distribution audit Stocks and control; transportation; warehousing	Distribution objectives, strategies	Distribution plan	
	Production audit Value analysis; engineering development; work study; quality control; labour; materials, plant and space utilization; production planning; factories	Production objectives, strategies	Production plan	
	Financial audit Credit, debt, cash flow and budgetary control; resource allocation; capital expenditure; long-term finance	Financial objectives, strategies	Financial plan	
	Personnel audit Management, technical and administrative ability, etc.	Personnel objectives, strategies		

with its current range of products in its current markets. Any projected gap can be filled by the various methods of product development or market extension.

Undoubtedly the most important and difficult of all stages in the corporate planning process is the third step, *objective and strategy setting*, since if this is not done properly, everything that follows is of little value.

Later on we will discuss marketing objectives and strategies in more detail. For now, the important point to make is that this is the time in the planning cycle when a compromise has to be reached between what is wanted by the several functional departments and what is practicable, given all the constraints that any company has. For example, it is no good setting a marketing objective of penetrating a new market, if the company does not have the production capacity to cope with the new business, and if capital is not available for whatever investment is necessary in additional capacity. At this stage, objectives and strategies will be set for five years, or for whatever the planning horizon is.

Step 4 involves producing detailed *plans* for one year, containing the responsibilities, timing and costs of carrying out the first year's objectives, and broad plans for the following years.

These plans can then be incorporated into the *corporate plan*, which will contain long-range corporate objectives, strategies, plans, profit and loss accounts, and balance sheets.

At this point it is worth noting that one of the main purposes of a corporate plan is to provide a long-term vision of what the company is or is striving to become, taking account of shareholder expectations, environmental trends, resource market trends, consumption market trends, and the distinctive competence of the company as revealed by the management audit. What this means in practice is that the corporate plan will contain the following elements:

Desired level of profitability
Business boundaries
— what kinds of products will be sold to what kinds of markets (marketing)
— what kinds of facilities will be developed (production and distribution)
— the size and character of the labour force (personnel)
— funding (finance)
Other corporate objectives, such as social responsibility, corporate image, stock market image, employer image, etc.

Such a corporate plan, containing projected profit and loss accounts and balance sheets, being the result of the process described above, is more likely to provide long-term stability for a company than plans based on a more intuitive process and containing forecasts which tend to be little more than extrapolations of previous trends.

The headquarters of one major multinational company with a sophisticated budgeting system used to receive 'plans' from all over the world and coordinate them in quantitative and cross-functional terms such as numbers of employees, units of sale, items of plant, square feet of production area, and so on, together with the associated financial implications. The trouble was that the whole complicated edifice was built on the initial sales forecasts, which were themselves little more than a time-consuming numbers game. The really key strategic issues relating to products and markets were lost in all the financial activity, which eventually resulted in grave operational and profitability problems.

Assumptions

Let us now return to the preparation of the marketing plan. If we refer again to the marketing planning process, and have completed our marketing audit and SWOT analysis, assumptions now have to be written.

There are certain key determinants of success in all companies about which assumptions have to be made before the planning process can proceed. It is really a question of standardizing the planning environment. For example, it would be no good receiving plans from two product managers, one of whom believed the market was going to increase by 10 per cent, while the other believed the market was going to decline by 10 per cent.

Examples of assumptions might be:

'With respect to the company's industrial climate, it is assumed that:
1 Industrial overcapacity will increase from 105 per cent to 115 per cent as new industrial plants come into operation.
2 Price competition will force price levels down by 10 per cent across the board.
3 A new product in the field of *x* will be introduced by our major competitor before the end of the second quarter.'

Assumptions should be few in number, and if a plan is possible irrespective of the assumptions made, then the assumptions are unnecessary.

Marketing objectives and strategies

The next step in marketing planning is the writing of marketing objectives and strategies, the key step in the whole process.

An *objective* is what you want to achieve. A *strategy* is how you plan to achieve your objectives. Thus, there can be objectives and strategies at all levels in marketing. For example, there can be advertising objectives and strategies, and pricing objectives and strategies.

However, the important point to remember about marketing objectives is that they are about *products* and *markets* only. Commonsense will confirm that it is only by selling something to someone that the company's financial goals can be achieved, and that advertising, pricing, service levels, and so on are the means (or strategies) by which we might succeed in doing this. Thus, pricing objectives, sales promotion objectives, advertising objectives and the like should not be confused with marketing objectives.

Marketing objectives are simply about one or more of the following:

Existing products in existing markets
New products for existing markets
Existing products for new markets
New products for new markets

They should be capable of measurement, otherwise they are not objectives. Directional terms such as 'maximize', 'minimize', 'penetrate', 'increase', etc. are only acceptable if quantitative measurement can be attached to them. Measurement should be in terms of sales volume, sterling, market share, percentage penetration of outlets, and so on.

Marketing strategies are the means by which marketing objectives will be achieved and generally are concerned with the four Ps, as follows:

Product The general policies for product deletions, modifications, additions design, packaging, etc.

Price The general pricing policies to be followed for product groups in market segments.

Place The general policies for channels and customer service levels.

Promotion The general policies for communicating with customers under the relevant headings, such as advertising, sales force, sales promotion, public relations, exhibitions, direct mail, etc.

Having completed this major planning task, it is normal at this stage to employ judgement, analogous experience, field tests, and so on, to test out the feasibility of the objectives and strategies in terms of market share, sales, costs, profits, and so on. It is also normally at this stage that alternative plans and mixes are delineated, if necessary.

Programmes

The general marketing strategies are now developed into specific sub-objectives, each supported by more detailed strategy and action statements.

A company organized according to functions might have an advertising plan, a sales promotion plan, a pricing plan, and so on.

A product-based company might have a product plan, with objectives, strategies and tactics for price, place and promotion as necessary.

A market or geographically based company might have a market plan, with objectives, strategies and tactics for the four Ps as necessary.

Likewise, a company with a few major customers might have a customer plan.

Any combination of the above might be suitable, depending on circumstances.

Use of marketing plans

A written marketing plan is the backcloth against which operational decisions are taken on an on-going basis. Consequently too much detail should not be attempted. Its major function is to determine where the company is now, where it wants to go to, and how to get there. It lies at the heart of a company's revenue-generating activities and from it flow all other corporate activities, such as the timing of the cash flow, the size and character of the labour force, and so on.

The marketing plan should be distributed on a 'need to know' basis only. Finally, the marketing plan should be used as an aid to effective management. It cannot be a substitute for it.

The marketing budget

It will be obvious from all of this that the setting of budgets becomes not only much easier, but the resulting budgets are more likely to be realistic and related to what the *whole* company wants to achieve rather than just one functional department.

The problem of designing a dynamic system for budget setting rather than the 'tablets of stone' approach, which is more common, is a major challenge to the marketing and financial directors of all companies.

The most satisfactory approach would be for a marketing director to justify all his marketing expenditure from a zero base each year against the tasks he wishes to accomplish. A little thought will confirm that this is exactly the approach recommended in this chapter. If these procedures are followed, a hierarchy of objectives is built up in such a way that every item of budgeted expenditure can be related directly back to the initial corporate financial objectives. For example, if sales promotion is a major means of achieving an objective in a particular market, when sales promotional items appear in the programme, each one has a specific purpose which can be related back to a major objective.

Doing it this way not only ensures that every item of expenditure is fully accounted for as part of a rational, objective and task approach, but also that when changes have to be made during the period to which the plan relates, such changes can be made in such a way that the least damage is caused to the company's long-term objectives.

The incremental marketing expense can be considered to be all costs that are incurred after the product leaves the factory, *other than* costs involved in physical distribution, the costs of which usually represent a discrete subset.

There is, of course, no textbook answer to problems relating to questions such as whether packaging should be a marketing or a production expense, and whether some distribution costs could be considered to be marketing costs. For example, insistence on high service levels results in high inventory carrying costs. Only commonsense will reveal workable solutions to issues such as these.

Under price, however, any form of discounting that reduces the expected gross income, such as promotional discounts, quantity discounts, royalty rebates, and so on, as well as sales commission and unpaid invoices, should be given the most careful attention as incremental marketing expenses.

Most obvious incremental marketing expenses will occur, however, under the heading *promotion* in the form of advertising, sales salaries and expenses, sales promotional expenditure, direct mail costs, and so on.

The important point about the measurable effects of marketing activity is that anticipated levels should be the result of the most careful analysis of what is required to take the company towards its goals, while the most careful attention should be paid to gathering all items of expenditure under appropriate headings. The healthiest way of treating these issues is a zero-based budgeting approach.

Application questions

1 Describe your company's marketing planning system in detail.
2 List the *good* things and the *bad* things about it.
3 Say how you think it could be improved.

3 The Marketing Planning Process: 2
Removing the Myths

In spite of the apparent simplicity and logic of the process described in the last chapter, marketing planning remains one of the most baffling subjects, both for academics and practitioners alike. The purpose of this chapter is to remove some of the myths which surround this very complex area of marketing management and to explain why much of what passes for marketing planning in industry is largely ineffective. These conclusions are based on a four-year study carried out at Cranfield into how two hundred British industrial goods companies carried out their marketing planning. Four hundred directors were interviewed, the companies being broadly representative of the complete spectrum of type and size of industrial company.

Marketing's contribution to business success in manufacturing, distribution or merchanting activities lies in its commitment to detailed analysis of future opportunities to meet customer needs and a wholly professional approach to selling to well-defined market segments those products or services that deliver the sought-after benefits. While prices and discounts are important, as are advertising and promotion, the link with engineering through the product is paramount.

Such a commitment and activities must not be mistaken for budgets and forecasts. Those of course we need and have already got. Our accounting colleagues have long since seen to that. No—put quite bluntly, the process of marketing planning is concerned with identifying what and to whom sales are going to be made in the longer term to give revenue budgets and sales forecasts any chance of achievement. Furthermore, chances of achievement are a function of how good our intelligence services are; and how well suited are our strategies; and how well we are led.

Ignorance of marketing planning and associated operational problems

The degree to which a company is able to cope with its operating environment is very much a function of the understanding it has of the marketing planning process as a means of sharpening the rationality and focus of all levels of management throughout the organization.

This requires further explanation. What most companies think of as planning systems are little more than forecasting and budgeting systems. These give impetus and direction to tackling the current operational problems of the business, but tend merely to project the current business unchanged into the future—something often referred to in management literature as 'tunnel vision'.

The problem with this approach is that because companies are dynamically evolving systems within a dynamically evolving business environment, some means of evaluation of the way in which the two interact has to be found in order that there should be a better matching between them. Otherwise, because of a general unpreparedness, a company will suffer increased pressures in the short term, in trying to react and to cope with environmental factors.

Many companies, having gone through various forms of rationalization or efficiency-increasing measures, become aware of the opportunities for making profit which have been lost to them because of their unpreparedness, but are confused about how to make better use of their limited resources. This problem increases in importance in relation to the size and diversity of companies.

In other words, there is widespread awareness of lost market opportunities through unpreparedness and real confusion over what to do about it. It is hard not to conclude, therefore, that there is a strong relationship between these two problems and the systems most widely in use at present, i.e. *sales forecasting and budgeting systems*.

Table 3.1 lists the most frequently mentioned operating problems resulting from a reliance on traditional sales forecasting and budgeting procedures in the absence of a marketing planning system.

It is not difficult to see the connection between all of these problems. However, what is perhaps not apparent from the list is that each of these operational difficulties is in fact a symptom of a much larger problem which emanates from the way in which the objectives of a firm are set.

The meaningfulness, hence the eventual effectiveness, of any objective, is heavily dependent on the quality of the informational inputs about the business environment. However, objectives also need to be realistic, and to be realistic, they have to be closely related to the firm's particular capabili-

Table 3.1   Most frequently mentioned problems

1   Lost opportunities for profit
2   Meaningless numbers in long-range plans
3   Unrealistic objectives
4   Lack of actionable market information
5   Interfunctional strife
6   Management frustration
7   Proliferation of products and markets
8   Wasted promotional expenditure
9   Pricing confusion
10 Growing vulnerability to environmental change
11 Loss of control over the business

ties in the form of its assets, competences and reputation that have evolved over a number of years.

The objective-setting process of a business, then, is central to its effectiveness. What the Cranfield research demonstrated conclusively is that it is inadequacies in the objective-setting process which lie at the heart of many of the problems of British companies. Since companies are based on the existence of markets, and since a company's sole means of making profit is to find and maintain profitable markets, then clearly setting objectives in respect of these markets is a key business function. If the process by which this key function is performed is inadequate in relation to the differing organizational settings in which it takes place, it follows that operational efficiency will be adversely affected.

Some kind of appropriate system has to be used to enable meaningful and realistic marketing objectives to be set. A frequent complaint is the preoccupation with short-term thinking and an almost total lack of what has been referred to as 'strategic thinking'. Another complaint is that plans consist largely of numbers, which are difficult to evaluate in any meaningful way, since they do not highlight and quantify opportunities, emphasize key issues, show the company's position clearly in its markets, or delineate the means of achieving the sales forecasts. Indeed, very often the actual numbers that are written down bear little relationship to any of these things. Sales targets for the sales force are often inflated in order to motivate them to higher achievement, while the actual budgets themselves are deflated in order to provide a safety net against shortfall. Both act as demotivators and both lead to the frequent use of expressions such as 'ritual', 'the numbers game', 'meaningless horsetrading', and so on. It is easy to see how the problems listed in Table 3.1 begin to manifest themselves in this sort of environment. Closely allied to this is the frequent reference to profit as being the only objective necessary to successful business performance.

This theme is frequently encountered. There is in the minds of many businessmen the assumption that in order to be commercially successful, all that is necessary is for 'the boss' to set profit targets, to decentralize the firm into groups of similar activities, and then to make managers accountable for achieving those profits.

However, even though many British companies have made the making of 'profit' almost the sole objective, many of our industries have gone into decline, and ironically there has also been a decline in real profitability. There are countless examples of companies pursuing decentralized profit goals that have failed miserably.

Why should this be so? It is largely because some top managers believe that all they have to do is to set profit targets, and somehow middle management will automatically make everything come right. Indeed, there is much evidence to show that many companies believe that planning is only about setting profit goals. However, while this is an easy task for any company to do, saying exactly *how* these results are to be achieved is altogether a different matter.

Here it is necessary to focus attention on what so many companies appear to be bad at, namely determining strategies for matching what the firm is good at with properly researched market-centred opportunities, and then scheduling and costing out what has to be done to achieve these objectives. There is little evidence of a deep understanding of what it is that companies can do better than their competitors or of how their distinctive competence can be matched with the needs of certain customer groups. Instead, overall volume increases and minimum rates of return on investment are frequently applied to all products and markets, irrespective of market share, market growth rate, or the longevity of the product life cycle. Indeed there is a lot of evidence to show that many companies are in trouble today precisely because their decentralized units manage their business only for the current profit and loss account, often at the expense of giving up valuable and hard-earned market share and running down the current business.

Thus, financial objectives, while being essential measures of the desired performance of a company, are of little practical help, since they say nothing about *how* the results are to be achieved. The same applies to sales forecasts and budgets, which are *not* marketing objectives and strategies. Understanding the real meaning and significance of marketing objectives helps managers to know what information they need to enable them to think through the implications of choosing one or more positions in the market. Finding the right words to describe the logic of marketing objectives and strategies is infinitely more difficult than writing down numbers on a piece of paper and leaving the strategies implicit. This lies at the heart of the problem. For clearly, a numbers-oriented system will not encourage managers to think in a structured way about strategically relevant market segments, nor will it encourage the collection, analysis and synthesis of actionable market data. And in the absence of such activities within operating units, it is unlikely that headquarters will have much other than intuition and 'feel' to use as a basis for decisions about the management of scarce resources.

This raises the difficult question of how these very complex problems can be overcome, for this is what baffles those who have been forced by market pressures to consider different ways of coping with their environment.

The problem remains of how to get managers throughout an organization to think beyond the horizon of the current year's operations. This applies universally to all types and sizes of company. Even chief executives of small companies find difficulty in breaking out of the fetters of the current profit and loss account.

The successes enjoyed in the past are often the result of the easy marketability of products, and during periods of high economic prosperity there was little pressure on companies to do anything other than solve operational problems as they arose. Careful planning for the future seemed unnecessary. However, most companies today find themselves in increasingly competitive markets, and there is a growing realization that success in the future will come only from patient and meticulous planning and market preparation. This entails making a commitment to the future.

The problem is that in large companies, managers who are evaluated and rewarded on the basis of current operations find difficulty in concerning themselves about the corporate future. This is exacerbated by behavioural issues, in the sense that it is safer, and more rewarding personally, for a manager to do what he knows best, which in most cases is to manage his *current* range of products and customers in order to make the *current* year's budget.

Unfortunately, long-range sales forecasting systems do not provide the answer. This kind of extrapolative approach fails to solve the problem of identifying precisely what has to be done today to ensure success in the future. Exactly the same problem exists in both large diversified companies and in small undiversified companies, except that in the former the problem is magnified and multiplied by the complexities of distance, hierarchical levels of management, and diversity of operations. Nevertheless, the problem is fundamentally the same.

Events that affect economic performance in a business come from so many directions, and in so many forms, that it is impossible for any manager to be precise about how they interact in the form of problems to be overcome, and opportunities to be exploited. The best a manager can do is to form a reasoned view about how they have affected the past, and how they will develop in the future, and what action needs to be taken over a period of time to enable the company to prepare itself for the expected changes. The problem is *how* to get managers to formulate their thoughts about these things, for until they have, it is unlikely that any objectives that are set will have much relevance or meaning.

Einstein wrote: 'The formulation of a problem is far more essential than its solution, which may be merely a matter of mathematical or experimental skill. To raise new questions, new possibilities, to regard old problems from a new angle, requires creative imagination.'

Unfortunately, such creativity is rare, especially when most managers are totally absorbed in managing today's business. Accordingly, they need some system which will help them to think in a structured way about problem formulation. It is the provision of such a rational framework to help them to make explicit their intuitive economic models of the business that is almost totally lacking from the forecasting and budgeting systems of most companies. It is apparent that in the absence of any such synthesized and simplified views of the business, setting meaningful objectives for the future seems like an insurmountable problem, and this in turn encourages the perpetuation of systems involving merely the extrapolation of numbers.

There is also substantial evidence that those companies that provide procedures for this process, in the form of standardized methods of presentation, have gone some considerable way to overcoming this problem. Although the possible number of analyses of business situations is infinite, procedural approaches help managers throughout an organization at least to consider the essential elements of problem definition in a structured way. This applies even to difficult foreign markets, where data and information are hard to come by, and even to markets which are being managed by agents, who find that these structured approaches, properly managed, help *their* businesses as well as those of their principals.

However, there are two further major advantages enjoyed by these companies. Firstly, the level of management frustration is lower and motivation is higher because the system provides a method of reaching agreement on such difficult matters as an assessment of the company's distinctive competence and the nature of the competitive environment. The internecine disputes and frustration which we all experience so often in our business lives is largely the result of an almost total absence of the means of discussing these issues and of reaching agreement on them. If a manager's boss does not understand what his environmental problems are, what his strengths and weaknesses are, nor what he is trying to achieve, and in the absence of any structured procedures and common terminology that can be used and understood by everybody, communications will be bad and the incidence of frustration will be higher.

Secondly, some form of standardized approach which is understood by all considerably improves the ability of headquarters management not only to understand the problems of individual operating units, but also to react to them in a constructive and helpful way. This is because they receive information in a way which enables them to form a meaningful overview of total company activities and this provides a rational basis for resource allocation.

To summarize, a structured approach to situation analysis is necessary, irrespective of the size or complexity of the organization. Such a system should:

1 Ensure that comprehensive consideration is given to the definition of strengths and weaknesses and to problems and opportunities.
2 Ensure that a logical framework is used for the presentation of the key issues arising from this analysis.

Very few companies in Britain have planning systems which possess these characteristics. Those that do, manage to cope with their environment more effectively than those that do not. They find it easier to set meaningful marketing objectives, are more confident about the future, enjoy greater control over the business, and react less on a piecemeal basis to ongoing events. In short, they suffer less operational problems and are as a result more effective organizations.

What is marketing planning?

Let us begin by reminding ourselves what it is. It is a logical sequence of activities leading to the setting of marketing objectives and the formulation of plans for achieving them. It is a management *process*.

Conceptually, the process is very simple and, in summary, comprises the steps outlined in Figure 2.1.

This process is universally agreed by the experts. Formalized marketing planning by means of a planning system is, *per se*, little more than a structured way of identifying a range of options, for the company, of making them explicit in writing, of formulating marketing objectives which are consistent with the company's overall objectives and of scheduling and costing out the specific activities most likely to bring about the achievement of the objectives. *It is the systematization of this process which is distinctive and was found to lie at the heart of the theory of marketing planning.*

Naivety about marketing planning

We have just rehearsed with you the notions that any textbook would offer should you care to re-read it. We have long been bemused, however, by the fact that many meticulous marketing planning companies fare badly while the sloppy or inarticulate in marketing terms do well. Is there any real relationship between marketing planning and commercial success? And, if so, how does that relationship work its way through?

There are, of course, many studies which identify a number of benefits to be obtained from marketing planning. But there is little explanation for the commercial success of those companies that do *not* engage in formalized planning. Nor is there much exploration of the circumstances of those commercially unsuccessful companies that also have formalized marketing planning systems, and where the dysfunctional consequences are recognized, there is a failure to link this back to any kind of theory.

'Success' is, of course, influenced by many factors apart from just planning procedures. For example:

1 Financial performance at any one point in time is not necessarily a reflection of the adequacy or otherwise of planning procedures (cf the hotel industry, location, tourism etc.).
2 Some companies just happen to be in the right place at the right time(s).
3 Companies have many and varied objectives, such as, for example, stylistic objectives.
4 There is a proven relationship between management style and commercial success.

In other words, marketing planning procedures *alone* are not enough for success.

We have said that the process of marketing planning is conceptually very simple and universally applicable. However, it is this very simplicity and universality that make it extremely complex once a number of contextual issues are added such as (a) company size; (b) degree of internationalization; (c) management style; (d) degree of business environmental turbulence and competitive hostility; (e) marketing growth rate; (f) market share; (g) technological changes; and so on.

It is very clear that the simplistic theories do not adequately address such contextual issues in relation to marketing planning, which may well account for the fact that so few companies actually do it.

In fact, 90 per cent of industrial goods companies in the Cranfield Study did not, by their own admission, produce anything approximating to an integrated, co-ordinated and internally consistent plan for their marketing activities. This included a substantial number of companies that had highly formalized procedures for marketing planning.

Certainly, few of these companies enjoyed the claimed benefits of formalized marketing planning, which in summary are as follows:

1 Co-ordination of the activities of many individuals whose actions are inter-related over time.
2 Identification of expected developments.
3 Preparedness to meet changes when they occur.
4 Minimization of non-rational responses to the unexpected.
5 Better communication among executives.
6 Minimization of conflicts among individuals which would result in a subordination of the goals of the company to those of the individual.

Indeed, many companies have a lot of the trappings of sophisticated marketing planning systems but suffer as many dysfunctional consequences as those companies that have only forecasting and budgeting systems. It is clear that for any marketing planning system to be effective, certain conditions have to be satisfied, which we shall deal with in detail shortly.

It should be pointed out, however, that it is by no means essential for any company not suffering from hostile and unstable competitive and environmental conditions to have an effective marketing planning system. Without exception, all those companies in the Cranfield Study which did not have an effective marketing planning system and which were profitable, were also operating in buoyant or high-growth markets. Such companies, though, were less successful than comparable companies with effective marketing planning systems. Success was considered to be not only a company's financial performance over a number of years, but also the way it coped with its environment.

What this means is that, apart from profitability, a company with an effective marketing planning system is likely to have:

Widely understood objectives
Highly motivated employees
High levels of actionable market information
Greater interfunctional co-ordination
Minimum waste and duplication of resources
Acceptance of the need for continuous change and a clear understanding of priorities
Greater control over the business and less vulnerability from the unexpected

In the case of companies without effective marketing planning systems, while it is possible to be profitable over a number of years, especially in high-growth markets, such companies will tend to be less profitable over time and to suffer problems which are the very opposite of the benefits referred to above.

Furthermore, companies without effective marketing planning systems tend to suffer more serious commercial organization consequences when environmental and competitive conditions become hostile and unstable.

None of these points are new, in the sense that most of these benefits and problems are discernable to the careful observer. They are, however, actionable propositions for marketers.

Marketing planning systems: design and implementation problems

Many companies currently under siege have recognized the need for a more structured approach to planning their marketing and have opted for the kind of standardized, formalized procedures written about so much in textbooks. These rarely bring the claimed benefits and often bring marketing planning itself into disrepute.

It is clear that any attempt at the introduction of formalized marketing planning systems has serious organizational and behavioural implications for a company, as it requires a change in its approach to managing its business. It is also clear that unless a company recognizes these implications, and plans to seek ways of coping with them, formalized marketing planning will be ineffective.

Marketing planning is in practice a complex process, proceeding as it does from reviews to objectives, strategies, programmes, budgets and back again, until some kind of acceptable compromise is reached between what is desirable, and what is practicable, given all the constraints that any company has.

It has been stated that the literature underestimates the operational difficulties of designing and implementing systems and procedures for marketing planning, and that the task becomes progressively more complex as the size and diversity of a company increases. Also, the literature is inadequate in the extent to which it provides practical guidance on design and implementation.

The Cranfield research included a number of examples of companies that had been forced by market pressures to initiate procedures to help top management gain better control over the business. In all such cases, those responsible for designing the system found very little of practical help, either in the literature or in management courses. Enormous difficulties in system design and implementation were encountered in every instance.

The purpose of this section is to discuss these design and implementation

problems. The most frequently encountered problems are summarized in
Table 3.2.

Table 3.2   Marketing planning systems: design and implementation problems

1	Weak support from chief executive and top management
2	Lack of a plan for planning
3	Lack of line management support

   — hostility
   — lack of skills
   — lack of information
   — lack of resources
   — inadequate organization structure

4	Confusion over planning terms
5	Numbers in lieu of written objectives and strategies
6	Too much detail, too far ahead
7	Once-a-year ritual
8	Separation of operational planning from strategic planning
9	Failure to integrate marketing planning into a total corporate planning system
10	Delegation of planning to a planner

Weak support from chief executive and top management

There can be no doubt that unless the chief executive sees the need for a
formalized marketing planning system, understands it, and shows an active
interest in it, it is virtually impossible for a senior functional marketing
executive to initiate procedures that will be used in a meaningful way.

This is particularly so in companies that are organized on the basis of
divisional management, for which the marketing executive has no profit
responsibility and in which he has no line management authority. In such
cases, it is comparatively easy for senior operational managers to create
'political' difficulties, the most serious of which is just to ignore the new
procedures entirely. Usually, however, the reasons for not participating in
or for only partially following instructions, centre around the issues summarized in Table 3.2.

The vital role that the chief executive and top management *must* play in
marketing planning underlines one of the key points in this section. That is,
that it is *people* who make systems work, and that system design and
implementation have to take account of the 'personality' of both the
organization and the people involved, and that these are different in all
organizations. One of the most striking features we have observed is the
difference in 'personalities' between companies, and the fact that within any
one company there is a marked similarity between the attitudes of executives. These attitudes vary from the impersonal, autocratic kind at one
extreme to the highly personal, participative kind at the other.

Any system, therefore, has to be designed around the people who have to make it work, and has to take account of the prevailing traditions, attitudes, skills, resource availability and organizational constraints. Since the chief executive and top management are the key influencers of these factors, without their active support and participation any formalized marketing planning system is unlikely to work. This fact emerged very clearly from the Cranfield research, the worst possible manifestation of which was the way in which chief executives and top managers ignored plans which emerged from the planning system and continued to make key decisions which appeared illogical to those who had participated in the production of the plans. This very quickly destroyed any credibility that the emerging plans might have had, led to the demise of the procedures, and to serious levels of frustration throughout the organization.

Indeed, there is some evidence leading to the belief that chief executives who fail, firstly, to understand the essential role of marketing in generating profitable revenue in a business, and, secondly, to understand how marketing can be integrated into the other functional areas of the business through marketing planning procedures, are a key contributory factor in poor economic performance. There is a depressing preponderance of accountants who live by the rule of 'the bottom line' and who apply universal financial criteria indiscriminately to all products and markets, irrespective of the long-term consequences. There is a similar preponderance of engineers who see marketing as an unworthy activity that is something to do with activities such as television advertising; and who think of their products only in terms of their technical features and functional characteristics, in spite of the overwhelming body of evidence that exists that these are only a part of what a customer buys. Not surprisingly, in companies headed by people like this, marketing planning is either non-existent, or where it is tried, it fails. This is the most frequently encountered barrier to effective marketing planning.

Lack of a plan for planning

The next most common cause of the failure or partial failure of marketing planning systems is the belief that, once a system is designed, it can be implemented immediately. One company achieved virtually no improvement in the quality of the plans coming into headquarters from the operating companies over a year after the introduction of a very sophisticated system. The evidence indicates that a period of around three years is required in a major company before a complete marketing planning system can be implemented according to its design.

Failure, or partial failure, then, is often the result of not developing a timetable for introducing a new system, to take account of the following:

1 The need to communicate why a marketing planning system is necessary.
2 The need to recruit top management support and participation.
3 The need to test the system out on a limited basis to demonstrate its effectiveness and value.
4 The need for training programmes, or workshops, to train line management in its use.
5 Lack of data and information in some parts of the world.
6 Shortage of resources in some parts of the world.

Above all, a resolute sense of purpose and dedication is required, tempered by patience and a willingness to appreciate the inevitable problems which will be encountered in its implementation.

This problem is closely linked with the third major reason for planning system failure, which is lack of line management support.

Lack of line management support

Hostility, lack of skills, lack of data and information, lack of resources, and an inadequate organizational structure, all add up to a failure to obtain the willing participation of operational managers.

Hostility on the part of line managers is by far the most common reaction to the introduction of new marketing planning systems. The reasons for this are not hard to find, and are related to the system initiators' lack of a plan for planning.

New systems inevitably require considerable explanation of the procedures involved and are usually accompanied by proformae, flow charts and the like. Often these devices are most conveniently presented in the form of a manual. When such a document arrives on the desk of a busy line manager, unheralded by previous explanation or discussion, the immediate reaction often appears to be fear of his possible inability to understand it and to comply with it, followed by anger, and finally rejection. He begins to picture headquarters as a remote 'ivory tower', totally divorced from the reality of the market place.

This is often exacerbated by his absorption in the current operating and reward system, which is geared to the achievement of *current* results, while the new system is geared to the future. Also, because of the trend in recent years towards the frequent movement of executives around organizations, there is less interest in planning for future business gains from which someone else is likely to benefit.

Allied to this is the fact that many line managers are ignorant of basic marketing principles, have never been used to breaking up their markets into strategically relevant segments, nor of collecting meaningful information about them.

This lack of skill is compounded by the fact that there are few countries in the world which match the wealth of useful information and data available in countries such as the USA and the UK. This applies particularly to rapidly-growing economies, where the limited aggregate statistics are not only unreliable and incomplete, but also quickly out of date. The seriousness of this problem is highlighted by the often rigid list of home office informational requirements, which is based totally on the home market.

The solution to this particular problem requires a good deal of patience, commonsense, ingenuity and flexibility on the part of both headquarters and operating management. This is closely connected with the need to consider resource availability and the prevailing organization structure. The problem of lack of reliable data and information can only be solved by devoting time and money to its solution, and where available resources are scarce, it is unlikely that the information demands of headquarters can be met.

It is for this reason that some kind of appropriate headquarters organization has to be found for the collection and dissemination of valuable information, and that training has to be provided on ways of solving this problem.

Again, these issues are complicated by the varying degrees of size and complexity of companies. It is surprising to see the extent to which organisational structures cater inadequately for marketing as a function. In small companies, there is often no one other than the sales manager, who spends all his time engaged either in personal selling or in managing the sales force. Unless the chief executive is marketing-oriented, marketing planning is just not done.

In medium sized and large companies, particularly those that are divisionalized, there is rarely any provision at board level for marketing as a discipline. Sometimes there is a commercial director, with line management responsibility for the operating divisions, but apart from sales managers at divisional level, or a marketing manager at head office level, marketing as a function is not particularly well catered for. Where there is a marketing manager, he tends to be somewhat isolated from the mainstream activities.

The most successful organizations are those with a fully integrated marketing function, whether it is line management responsible for sales, or a staff function, with operating units being a microcosm of the head office organization.

However, it is clear that without a suitable organizational structure, any attempt to implement a marketing planning system which requires the collection, analysis and synthesis of market-related information, is unlikely to be successful. A classic example of this was a large diversified multinational, where no provision was made at headquarters for marketing, other than through the divisional directors, and where divisions also generally had no marketing function other than sales management. Their first attempt at writing a strategic plan as a result of market pressures was a complete failure.

The problem of organizing for marketing planning is discussed further in Chapter 11.

Confusion over planning terms

Confusion over planning terms is another reason for the failure of marketing planning systems. The initiators of these systems, often highly qualified, frequently use a form of planning terminology that is perceived by operational managers as meaningless jargon. One company even referred to the Ansoff matrix, and made frequent references to other forms of matrices, missions, dimensions, quadrants, and so on.

Those companies with successful planning systems try to use terminology which will be familiar to operational management, and where terms such as 'objectives' and 'strategies' are used, these are clearly defined, with examples given of their practical use.

At the end of Chapter 12 there is a glossary of terms.

Numbers in lieu of written objectives and strategies

Most managers in operating units are accustomed to completing sales forecasts, together with the associated financial implications. They are not accustomed to considering underlying causal factors for past performance or expected results, nor of highlighting opportunities, emphasizing key issues, and so on. Their outlook is essentially parochial and short-term, with a marked tendency to extrapolate numbers and to project the current business unchanged into the next fiscal year.

Thus, when a marketing planning system suddenly requires that they should make explicit their implicit economic model of the business, they cannot do it. So, instead of finding words to express the logic of their objectives and strategies, they repeat their past behaviour and fill in the data sheets provided without any narrative.

It is the provision of data sheets, and the emphasis which the system places on the physical counting of things, that encourages the questionnaire-completion mentality and hinders the development of the creative analysis so essential to effective strategic planning.

Those companies with successful marketing planning systems ask only for essential data and place greater emphasis on narrative to explain the underlying thinking behind the objectives and strategies.

Too much detail, too far ahead

Connected with this is the problem of over-planning, usually caused by elaborate systems that demand information and data that headquarters do not need and can never use. Systems that generate vast quantities of paper are generally demotivating for all concerned.

The biggest problem in this connection is undoubtedly the insistence on a detailed and thorough marketing audit. In itself this is not a bad discipline to impose on managers, but to do so without also providing some guidance on how it should be summarized to point up the key issues merely leads to the production of vast quantities of useless information. Its uselessness stems from the fact that it robs the ensuing plans of focus and confuses those who read it by the amount of detail provided.

The trouble is that few managers have the creative or analytical ability to isolate the really key issues, with the result that far more problems and opportunities are identified than the company can ever cope with. Consequently, the truly key strategic issues are buried deep in the detail and do not receive the attention they deserve until it is too late.

In a number of companies with highly detailed and institutionalized marketing planning systems, the resulting plans contain so much detail that it is impossible to identify what the major objectives and strategies are. Also, the managers in these companies are rarely able to express a simplified view of the business or of the essential things that have to be done today to ensure success. Such companies are often over-extended, trying to do too many things at once. Over-diversity and being extended in too many directions, makes control over a confusingly heterogeneous portfolio of products and markets extremely difficult.

In companies with successful planning systems, there is at all levels a widespread understanding of the key objectives that have to be achieved, and of the means of achieving them. In such companies, the rationale of each layer of the business is clear, and actions and decisions are disciplined by clear objectives that hang logically together as part of a rational, overall purpose.

The clarity and cohesiveness is achieved by means of a system of 'layering'. At each successive level of management throughout the organization, lower-level analyses are synthesized into a form that ensures that only the essential information needed for decision-making and control purpose reaches the next level of management. Thus, there are hierarchies of audits, SWOT analyses, assumptions, objectives, strategies and plans. This means, for example, that at conglomerate headquarters, top management have a clear understanding of the really key macro issues of company-wide significance, while at the lower level of profit responsibility, management also have a clear understanding of the really key micro issues of significance to the unit.

It can be concluded that a good measure of the effectiveness of a company's marketing planning system is the extent to which different managers in the organization can make a clear, lucid and logical statement about the major problems and opportunities they face, how they intend to deal with these, and how what they are doing fits in with some greater overall purpose.

Once-a-year ritual

One of the commonest weaknesses in the marketing planning systems of those companies whose planning systems fail to bring the expected benefits, is the ritualistic nature of the activity. In such cases, operating managers treat the writing of the marketing plan as a thoroughly irksome and unpleasant duty. The proformae are completed, not always very diligently, and the resulting plans are quickly filed away, never to be referred to again. They are seen as something which is required by headquarters rather than as an essential tool of management. In other words, the production of the marketing plan is seen as a once-a-year ritual, a sort of game of management bluff. It is not surprising that the resulting plans are not used.

While this is obviously closely related to the explanations already given as to why some planning systems are ineffective, a common feature of companies that treat marketing planning as a once-a-year ritual is the short lead time given for the completion of the process. The problem with this approach is that in the minds of managers it tends to be relegated to a position of secondary importance.

In companies with effective systems, the planning cycle will start in March or April and run through to September or October, with the total twelve-month period being used to evaluate the on-going progress of existing plans by means of the company's marketing intelligence system. Thus, by spreading the planning activity over a longer period, and by means of the active participation of all levels of management at the appropriate moment, planning becomes an accepted and integral part of management behaviour rather than an addition to it which calls for unusual behaviour. There is a much better chance that plans resulting from such a system will be formulated in the sort of form that can be converted into things that people are actually going to do.

Separation of operational planning from strategic planning

This sub-section must be seen against the background of the difficulty which the majority of British companies experience in carrying out any meaningful strategic planning. In the majority of cases, the figures that appear in the long-term corporate plan are little more than statistical extrapolations that satisfy boards of directors. If they are not satisfactory, the numbers are just altered, and frequently the gap between where a company gets to compared with where it had planned to be in real terms, grows wider over time.

Nevertheless most companies make long-term projections. Unfortunately, in the majority of cases these are totally separate from the short-term planning activity that takes place largely in the form of forecasting and budgeting. The view that they should be separate is supported by many of the writers in this field, who describe strategic planning as very different, and therefore divorced, from operational planning. Indeed, many stress that failure to understand the essential difference between the two leads to confusion and prevents planning from becoming an integrated part of the company's overall management system. Yet it is precisely this separation between short- and long-term plans which the Cranfield research revealed as being the major cause of the problems experienced today by many of the respondents. It is the failure of long-term plans to determine the difficult choices between the emphasis to be placed on current operations and the development of new business that leads to the failure of operating management to consider any alternatives to what they are currently doing.

The almost total separation of operational or short-term planning from strategic or long-term planning is a feature of many companies whose systems are not very effective.

More often than not, the long-term strategic plans tend to be straight-line extrapolations of past trends, and because different people are often involved, such as corporate planners, to the exclusion of some levels of operating management, the resulting plans bear virtually no relationship to the more detailed and immediate short-term plans.

This separation positively discourages operational managers from thinking strategically, with the result that detailed operational plans are completed in a vacuum. The so-called strategic plans do not provide the much-needed cohesion and logic, because they are seen as an ivory tower exercise which contains figures in which no one really believes.

Unless strategic plans are built up from sound strategic analysis at grass-roots level by successive layers of operational management, they have little realism as a basis for corporate decisions. At the same time, operational plans will become increasingly parochial in their outlook and will fail to incorporate the decisions that have to be taken today to safeguard the future.

Operational planning, then, should very much be part of the strategic planning process, and vice versa. Indeed, wherever possible, they should be completed at the same time, using the same managers and the same informational inputs.

The detailed operational plan should be the first year of the long-term plan, and operational managers should be encouraged to complete their long-term projections at the same time as their short-term projections. The advantage is that it encourages managers to think about what decisions have to be made in the current planning year, in order to achieve the long-term projections.

Failure to integrate marketing planning into a total corporate planning system

It is difficult to initiate an effective marketing planning system in the absence of a parallel corporate planning system. This is yet another facet of the separation of operational planning from strategic planning. For unless similar processes and time scales to those being used in the marketing planning system are also being used by other major functions such as Distribution, Production, Finance and Personnel, the sort of trade-offs and compromises that have to be made in any company between what is wanted and what is practicable and affordable, will not take place in a rational way. These trade-offs have to be made on the basis of the fullest possible understanding of the reality of the company's multifunctional strengths and weaknesses, and opportunities and threats.

One of the problems of systems in which there is either a separation of the strategic corporate planning process or in which marketing planning is the only formalized system, is the lack of participation of key functions of the company, such as engineering or production. Where these are key determinants of success, as in capital goods companies, a separate marketing planning system is virtually ineffective.

Where marketing, however, is a major activity, as in fast-moving industrial goods companies, it is possible to initiate a separate marketing planning system. The indications are that when this happens successfully, similar systems for other functional areas of the business quickly follow suit because of the benefits which are observed by the chief executive.

Delegation of planning to a planner

The incidence of this is higher with corporate planning than with marketing planning, although where there is some kind of corporate planning function at headquarters, and no organizational function for marketing, whatever strategic marketing planning takes place is done by the corporate planners as part of a system which is divorced from the operational planning mechanism. Not surprisingly, this exacerbates the separation of operational planning from strategic planning and encourages short-term thinking in the operational units.

Very often, corporate planners are young, highly qualified people, attached to the office of the chairman or group chief executive. They appear to be widely resented and are largely ignored by the mainstream of the business. There is not much evidence that they succeed in clarifying the company's overall strategy and there appears to be very little account taken of such strategies in the planning and thinking of operational units. The literature sees the planner basically as a co-ordinator of the planning, not as an initiator of goals and strategies. It is clear that without the ability and the willingness of operational management to co-operate, a planner becomes little more than a kind of headquarters administrative assistant. In many large companies, where there is a person at headquarters with the specific title of marketing planning manager, he has usually been appointed as a result of the difficulty of controlling businesses that have grown rapidly in size and diversity, and which present a baffling array of new problems to deal with.

His tasks are essentially those of system design and co-ordination of inputs, although he is also expected to formulate overall objectives and strategies for the board. In all cases, it is lack of line management skills and inadequate organizational structures that frustrates the company's marketing efforts, rather than inadequacies on the part of the planner. This puts the onus on the planner himself to do a lot of the planning, which is, not surprisingly, largely ineffective.

Two particularly interesting facts emerged from the Cranfield research. Firstly, the marketing planning manager, as the designer and initiator of systems for marketing planning, is often in an impossibly delicate political position *vis à vis* both his superior line managers and more junior operational managers. It is clear that not too many chief executives understand the role of planning and have unrealistic expectations of the planner, whereas for his part the planner cannot operate effectively without the full understanding, co-operation and participation of top management, and this rarely happens. Often, the appointment of a marketing planning manager, and sometimes of a senior marketing executive, seems to be an easier step for the chief executive and his board to take than giving serious consideration themselves to the implications of the new forces affecting the business and reformulating an overall strategy.

This leads on naturally to a second point. For the inevitable consequence of employing a marketing planning manager is that he will need to initiate changes in management behaviour in order to become effective. Usually these are far-reaching in their implications, affecting training, resource allocation, and organizational structures. As the catalyst for such changes, the planner, not surprisingly, comes up against enormous political barriers, the result of which is that he often becomes frustrated and eventually ineffective. This is without doubt a major problem, particularly for big companies. The problems which are raised by a marketing planning manager occur directly as a result of the failure of top management to give thought to the formulation of overall strategies. They have not done this in the past because they have not felt the need. However, when market pressures force the emerging problems of diversity and control to the surface, without a total willingness on their part to participate in far-reaching changes, there really is not much that a planner can do.

This raises the question again of the key role of the chief executive in the whole business of marketing planning. Without both his support and understanding of the very serious implications of initiating effective marketing planning procedures, whatever efforts are made, whether by a planner or a line manager, they will be largely ineffective.

Requisite marketing planning systems

The implications of all this are principally as follows:

1   Any closed loop marketing planning system (but especially one that is essentially a forecasting and budgeting system) will lead to a gradual decline of marketing and creativity. Therefore, there has to be some mechanism for preventing inertia from setting in through the over-bureaucratization of the system.
2   Marketing planning undertaken at the functional level of marketing, in the absence of a means of integration with other functional areas of the business at general management level, will be largely ineffective.
3   The separation of responsibility for operational and strategic marketing planning will lead to a divergence of the short-term thrust of a business at the operational level from the long-term objectives of the enterprise as a whole. This will encourage a preoccupation with short-term results at operational level, which normally makes the firm less effective in the long term.
4   Unless the chief executive understands and takes an active role in marketing planning, it will never be an effective system.
5   A period of up to three years is necessary (especially in large firms), for the successful introduction of an effective marketing planning system.

In the last chapter of this book we will explore in detail what is meant by the term 'requisite marketing planning' when we explain how to design and implement an effective marketing planning system.

For now, we believe we have given sufficient background information about the *process* of marketing planning, and why this apparently simple process requires much more perception and attention than is typically accorded it. We can now go on to explore in more detail each of the elements of this process before putting all the pieces together again in the final chapter.

Application questions

1   Taking each of the issues listed in Tables 3.1 and 3.2, say in what ways:
    (a) they apply to your company;
    (b) you deal successfully with them.

4 Completing the Marketing Audit: 1
The Customer and Market Audit

Now we understand the *process* of marketing planning, we can begin to look in more detail at its principal components. We have, as it were, seen the picture on the front of the jigsaw puzzle; we can now examine the individual pieces with a better understanding of where they fit.

The next two chapters are designed to help us to carry out a meaningful marketing audit. We have already looked at the issues that need to be considered; what we need now are the means to help us to undertake such an analysis.

It should be stressed that, while the following two chapters deal specifically with how to carry out a customer, market, and product audit, it should not be assumed that, in carrying out a marketing audit, price, promotion, and place, information and organization, are unimportant. Indeed, Chapters 7–11 are devoted to these important determinants of commercial success and will provide the marketing auditor with the necessary confidence to carry out these specific parts of the audit.

The difference between customers and consumers

We now turn our attention to one of the key determinants of successful marketing planning—*market segmentation*. This is fundamental to the matching process described in Chapter 1. But, in order to understand market segmentation, it is first necessary to appreciate the difference between *customers* and *consumers*, the meaning of *market share* and the phenomenon known as the *Pareto effect*.

Let us start with the difference between customers and consumers. The term 'consumer' is interpreted by most to mean the final consumer, who is not necessarily the customer. Take the example of the housewife who is

50

buying breakfast cereals. The chances are she is an intermediate customer, acting as an agent on behalf of the eventual consumers (her family) and, in order to market cereals effectively, it is clearly necessary to understand what the end-consumer wants, as well as what the housewife wants.

This is only relevant in that it is always necessary to be aware of the needs of eventual consumers down the buying chain. Consider the case of the industrial purchasing officer buying raw materials such as wool tops for conversion into semi-finished cloths which are then sold to other companies for incorporation into the final product, say a suit, or a dress, for sale in consumer markets. Here we can see that the requirements of those various intermediaries and the end-user himself are eventually translated into the specifications of the purchasing officer to the raw materials manufacturer. Consequently, the market needs that this manufacturing company is attempting to satisfy must in the last analysis be defined in terms of the requirements of the ultimate user—the consumer—even though our direct customer is quite clearly the purchasing officer.

Given that we can appreciate the distinction between customers and consumers and the need constantly to be alert to any changes in the ultimate consumption patterns of the products to which our own contributes, the next question to be faced is: who are our customers? Closely related to this question is the difficult issue of what our market share is.

What is our market share?

This question of market share is a key concept in marketing management, and we shall keep on returning to it. In the next chapter we will discuss why market share is important to a company. For now, let us confine ourselves to the question of what we mean when we talk about market share.

Firstly, a firm needs to be concerned with its share (or its proportion of volume or value) of an *actual* market rather than with a *potential* market. However, in order to measure an actual market, great care must be taken to ensure that we are measuring the right things. Take the example of the company manufacturing a nylon carpet for offices. It is clearly nonsense to include concrete in our measurement of the floor-covering market, because concrete, although a floor covering, does not satisfy the needs consumers have for warmth and colour, and therefore this is not a part of our market. But neither would it make sense to include, say, bedroom carpets made of wool. So we would probably end up with a definition of our market as the aggregate of all carpets of a certain fibre type sold into institutional outlets.

To help with this, the following definitions are useful:

Product class, e.g. cigarettes
Product form, e.g. filter
Product brand, e.g. Guards

Guards as a brand, for the purpose of measuring market share, is only *concerned with the aggregate of all other brands that satisfy the same group of customer wants.* Nevertheless, the manufacturer of Guards also needs to be aware of the sales trends of filter cigarettes and the cigarette market in total.

One of the most frequent mistakes that is made by people who do not understand what market share really means, is to assume that their company has only a small share of some market, whereas if the company is commercially successful it probably has a much larger share of a smaller market. Which brings us to another fascinating and extremely useful observation about markets.

Pareto effect

It is a phenomenon commonly observed by most companies that a small proportion of their customers account for a large proportion of their business. This is often referred to as the 80/20 rule, or the Pareto effect, whereby about 20 per cent of customers account for about 80 per cent of business.

Let us say that we graph the proportion of customers that account for a certain proportion of sales, then we might expect to find a relationship similar to that shown in Figure 4.1. Here customers have been categorized simply as A, B or C according to the proportion of sales they account for. The A customers, perhaps 25 per cent of the total, account for about 70 per cent of sales, B customers, say 55 per cent of the total, account for 20 per cent of total sales; and C customers, 20 per cent of the total, account for the remaining 10 per cent of sales.

The Pareto effect is found in almost all markets, from capital industrial goods to banking and consumer goods. What is the significance of this?

What is certain is that it does not mean that a company should drop 80 per cent of its customers. For one thing the sales volume bought by these customers makes a valuable contribution to overheads. For another, it is almost certain that the 80/20 rule would still apply to the remaining 20 per cent. One could go on forever until there was only a single customer left! However, in carrying out this kind of analysis, it should become obvious where the company should be placing its greatest effort.

There is, however, a serious danger. This form of analysis is static. In other words, the best potential customers may well be in the 80 per cent, or even in the larger group of non-customer.

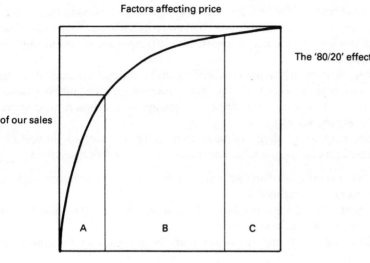

Figure 4.1

It is obvious then, that while such analysis is vital, great care is necessary over how it is used. This is something we can now begin to discuss.

One manufacturer in the soft drinks industry did an analysis of its trade in the south-east of England and found that almost 85 per cent of its trade was coming from 20 per cent of its customers. Yet exactly the same service was being given to them all. All were receiving fortnightly calls from the sales force, all received a fortnightly delivery, and all paid the same price for the product. Not surprisingly, this led to an enormous investment in depots and vehicles, while the associated operating expenses were out of all proportion to the margins enjoyed by the company. In this case, there was a simple answer. Most of the small accounts were handed over to a grateful whole-saler, which freed valuable capital and management time to concentrate on the really important areas of the business. Meanwhile, the company's pricing policy was revised to reward those customers who bought more, and the sales force was now free to concentrate on developing its existing business and on opening new profitable outlets.

Market segmentation

We can now begin to concentrate on one of the key concepts of marketing—market segmentation, which is the means by which any company seeks to gain a differential advantage over its competitors. Markets usually fall into natural groups, or segments, which contain customers who exhibit the same broad characteristics. These segments form separate markets in themselves and can often be of considerable size. Taken to its extreme, each individual consumer is a unique market segment, for all people are different in their requirements.

However, it is clearly uneconomical to make unique products for the needs of individuals, except in the most unusual circumstances. Consequently, products are made to appeal to groups of customers who share approximately the same needs.

It is not surprising, then, to hear that there are certain universally accepted criteria concerning what constitutes a viable market segment:

Segments should be of an adequate size to provide the company with an adequate return for its effort.

Members of each segment should have a high degree of similarity, yet be distinct from the rest of the market.

Criteria for describing segments must be relevant to the purchase situation.

Segments must be reachable.

While many of these criteria are obvious when we consider them, in practice market segmentation is one of the most difficult of marketing concepts to turn into a reality. Yet we must succeed, otherwise we become just another company selling what are called 'me too' products. In other words, what we offer the potential customer is very much the same as what any other company offers, and in such circumstances, it is likely to be the lowest priced article that is bought. This can be ruinous to our profits, unless we happen to have lower costs, hence higher margins than our competitors. There is more about this important aspect of marketing in Chapter 5.

There are basically two approaches to market segmentation, both of which have to be considered:

Analysis of customer responses or behaviour

Analysis of customer characteristics or attributes

Analysis of customer behaviour

This is essentially the manifestation of the way customers actually behave in the market place, and falls into two parts: firstly, *what* is bought; secondly, *why*.

In respect of *what* is bought, we are really talking about the actual structure of markets in the form of volume, value, the physical characteristics of products, place of purchase, frequency of purchase, price paid, and so on. This tells us if there are any groups of products (our outlets, or price categories, etc.) which are growing, static, or declining, i.e. where the opportunities are and where the problems are. For example, one carpet company whose sales were declining discovered on analysis that although the market in total was rising, the particular outlets to which they had traditionally sold, were accounting for a declining proportion of total market sales. Furthermore, demand for higher priced products was falling, as were the particular fibre types manufactured by this company. All this added up to a decline in sales and profitability, and led the company to change its emphasis towards some of the growing sectors of the market.

This is market segmentation at its most elementary level, yet it is surprising to find even today how many companies run apparently sophisticated budgeting systems which are based on little more than crude extrapolations of past sales trends and which leave the marketing strategies implicit. Such systems are usually the ones which cause serious commercial problems when market structures change as in the case of the carpet company. In this case the company changed direction too late and went bankrupt.

The same fate befell a shoe manufacturer who doggedly stuck to manufacturing the same products, in the same material, for the same kind of outlets, irrespective of the rapid changes that were taking place in the market.

The second part of analysing customer behaviour is trying to understand *why* customers behave the way they do, for surely if we can explain the behaviour of our customers, we are in a better position to sell to them.

Basically there are two principal theories of customer behaviour. One theory refers to the rational customer, who seeks to maximize his satisfaction or utility. His behaviour is determined by the utility derived from a purchase at the margin compared with his financial outlay and other opportunities foregone. While such a view of customers provides some important insights into behaviour, it must be remembered that many markets do not work this way at all, there being many examples of a growth in demand with every rise in price.

Another view of customer behaviour which helps to explain this phenomenon is that which describes the psycho-socio- customer, whose attitudes and behaviour are affected by family, work, prevailing cultural patterns, reference groups, his perceptions, aspirations, and 'life style'.

While such theories also provide useful insights, they rarely explain the totality of customer behaviour. For example, it is interesting to know that opinion leaders are often the first to adopt new ideas and new products, but unless these people can be successfully identified and communicated with, this information is of little practical use to us.

The most useful and practical way of explaining customer behaviour has been found to be *benefit segmentation*, i.e. the benefits sought by customers when they buy a product. For example, some customers buy products for their functional characteristics (product), for economy (price), for convenience and availability (place), for emotional reasons (promotion), or for a combination of these reasons (a trade-off). Otherwise, how else can the success of firms like Rolls-Royce, Harrods, and many others be explained? Understanding the benefits sought by customers helps us to organize our marketing mix in the way most likely to appeal to our target market. The importance of product benefits will become clearer in Chapter 5 in our discussion of product management.

'Customers don't buy products; they seek to acquire benefits.' This is the guiding principle of the marketing director of one of Britain's more innovative companies in the hair-care business. Behind that statement lies a basic principle of successful marketing. When people purchase products, they are not motivated in the first instance by physical features or objective attributes of the product but by the benefit that those attributes bring with them.

To take an example from industrial marketing, a purchaser of industrial cutting oil is not buying the particular blend of chemicals sold by leading manufacturers of industrial lubricants; rather, he is buying a bundle of benefits which includes the solving of a specific lubrication problem.

The difference between benefits and products is not just a question of semantics. It is crucial to the company seeking success. Every product has its features: size, shape, performance, weight, the material from which it is made, and so on. Many companies fall into the trap of talking to customers about these features rather than what those features mean to the customer. This is not surprising. For example, if, when asked a question about the product, the salesman could not provide an accurate answer, the customer might lose confidence and, doubting the salesman, will soon doubt his product. Most salesmen are therefore very knowledgeable about the technical features of the products they sell. They have to have these details at their fingertips when they talk to buyers, designers and technical experts.

However, being expert in technical detail is not enough. The customer may not be able to work out the benefits which particular features bring and it is therefore up to the salesman to explain the benefits which accrue from every feature he mentions.

A simple formula to ensure that this customer-oriented approach is adopted is always to use the phrase *'which means that'* to link a feature to the benefit it brings:

'Maintenance time has been reduced from 4 to 3 hours *which means that* most costs are reduced by . . .'

'The engine casing is made of aluminium *which means that* six more units can be carried on a standard truck load, *which means that* transport costs are reduced by . . .'

'The size of the quench tank has been increased by 25 per cent *which means that* on oil purchases alone you will save £2,000 in a year.'

'The new spherical bearing has self-aligning symmetrical rollers *which means that* the rollers find their own equilibrium, with the load always symmetrically distributed along the length of the roller, *which means* an extended life capacity.'

Benefit analysis

A company must undertake a detailed analysis to determine the full range of benefits they have to offer their customers. This can be done by listing the features of major products, together with what they mean to the customer. The analysis will produce various classes of benefit, outlined below.

Standard benefits

These are the basic benefits which arise from the features of the company and its products.

Every benefit must be listed. Care is needed to produce a comprehensive list. Because marketing staff are very familiar with the company and its products, they may take some features for granted. They must not fall into this trap when undertaking benefit analysis.

Buyers are rarely as knowledgeable as they appear and the company must make sure they include benefits which are neither unique nor overtly special; some of these benefits may even be offered by competitors.

Double benefits

A company will often be able to identify double benefits. For example, they may be selling a product which will bring benefits to their customer and, through an improvement in the customer's product, to the end-user:

'Our microcomputer has a range of software options to suit a wide variety of business uses *which means that*:
— the product will appeal to a wide variety of customers;
— customers will be able to purchase software which meets their particular needs.'

In the above example, the first benefit applies to the customer because it widens his potential market, and the second benefit applies to the potential end-user.

Company benefits

The customer rarely simply buys a product; he buys a relationship with his supplier. Factors such as delivery, credit, after-sales service, the location of depots and offices, reputation, and so on are all relevant to the customer. The benefit analysis should therefore examine the company and back-up services it offers. Typical company benefits include:

> 'We can offer a 24-hour delivery service because we have a national network of depots *which means that* you will never lose production due to delivery delays.'

> 'We are a large international corporation *which means that* you can rely on a comprehensive service throughout the world.'

> 'You can be sure of individual attention from us because we are a small family business.'

Differential benefits

Without doubt, however, while it is important for the industrial salesmen to go through this process of benefit analysis most thoroughly, it is vital that in doing it *differential* benefits compared with those of major competitors are identified. If a company cannot identify any differential benefits, then either what they are offering is identical to their competitors' offerings (which is unlikely) or they have not done the benefit analysis properly. It is important to make a particular note of differential benefits, for it is in these that the greatest chance of success lies.

Analysis of customer attributes

This seeks to find some way of describing the customer groups located in our previous analysis for the purpose of communicating with them. For clearly, however clever we have been in isolating segments, unless we can find some way of describing them such that we can address them through our communication programme, our efforts will have been to no avail.

Demographic descriptors have been found to be the most useful method for this purpose. For consumer markets, this is age, sex, education, stage in the family life cycle, and socio-economic groupings (A, B, C1, C2, D, E). This latter method describes people by their social status in life as represented by their jobs. Not surprisingly, A, B and C categories, which include most of the professions and senior managers, are light television viewers; consequently if they are your target market it does not make much sense to advertise your product or service on television. However, they can be effectively reached by means of certain newspapers and magazines, where they comprise the principal readership.

From this it will be gathered that there is a very useful correlation between readership and viewing patterns and these socio-economic groupings, and this can be most useful in helping us to communicate cost-effectively with our target market by means of advertising. Obviously, however, if we have no real idea of who our target market is, then we are unlikely to be able to take advantage of this convenient method.

It is obvious that at different stages in the family cycle, we have different needs, and this can be another most useful way of describing our market. Banks and insurance companies have been particularly adept at developing products specially for certain age categories.

For industrial markets, SIC (Standard Industrial Classification) categories, number of employees, turnover and production processes, have been found to be useful demographic descriptors.

Table 4.1 provides a useful summary of all these issues relating to market segmentation.

Table 4.1   Bases for market segmentation

What is bought	Volume
	Price
	Outlets
	Physical characteristics
	Geography
Who buys	Demographic
	Socio-economic
	Brand loyalty
	Heavy/light users
	Personality, traits, life styles
Why	Benefits
	Attitudes
	Perceptions
	Preferences

Some examples

Since we have stated that market segmentation is the key to commercial success, perhaps we should give some examples of market segmentation in practice.

The first example concerns an oil company trying unsuccessfully to compete in the industrial lubricants market in Europe. It found that it was always beaten on price. It soon became obvious that it stood little chance of beating its competitors on price, in view of their vastly superior refining capacity, which gave economies of scale beyond the reach of this much smaller company.

Detailed analysis revealed that there were certain high-technology and innovative production processes that were much more concerned with high-quality technical solutions to their lubrication and cleansing problems than with price. These were confined to certain industrial classifications and to certain types of production processes within them. The company found that it had the technical skills to out-perform its larger competitors in these areas. Subsequently it trained its sales force to deal with these special customer groups and further directed its promotional campaigns at its new target market. The result was a company that could compete profitably in a market where previously it had experienced serious profitability problems.

Another company found itself competing unsuccessfully and unprofitably in the motor components market, against a European giant. It too found that it could only compete successfully by concentrating on the problem of certain types of original equipment manufacturer where price was not the major concern. It soon discovered that there were many opportunities for products manufactured to very high technical specifications, in which the technical reputation of the supplier was more important than the price charged.

Finally, the example of the segmentation of the toothpaste market illustrated in Table 4.2 shows how this market breaks down into a number of discrete groupings. It illustrates how unlikely it would be for any company trying to compete in this market to succeed unless they had such an in-depth understanding of the needs of each of these different customer groups. It also illustrates how some of the different methods of market segmentation described in this chapter can be combined to aid understanding of a market. It is clear how this knowledge can be translated into product formulations, packaging policies, sales promotion policies, media strategy, advertising copy, and so on. Without this kind of knowledge, it would be extremely difficult to develop any kind of meaningful marketing policy.

Why market segmentation is vital in marketing planning

In today's highly competitive world, few companies can afford to compete only on price, for the product has not yet been sold that someone, somewhere, cannot sell cheaper. Apart from which, in many markets it is rarely the cheapest product that succeeds anyway. This is an issue we will return to in the module dealing with the pricing plan. What this means is that we have

Table 4.2   Toothpaste market segmentation

	Sensory segment	Sociables	Worriers	Independent segment
Principal benefit sought	flavour, product appearance	brightness of teeth	decay prevention	price
Demographic strengths	children	teens, young people	large families	men
Behavioural characteristics	users of spearmint flavour	smokers	heavy users	heavy users
Brands favoured	Colgate Stripe	Macleans Plus White Ultra Bright	Crest	brands on sale
Personality characteristics	high self-involvement	high sociability	high hypo-chondriasis	high autonomy
Life style characteristics	hedonistic	active	conservative	value orientated

From Russell Haley 'Benefit segmentation: a decision-oriented research tool'. *Journal of Marketing*, Vol. 32, July 1968.

to find some way of differentiating ourselves from the competition, and the answer lies in *market segmentation*.

The truth is, very few companies can afford to be 'all things to all men'. The main aim of market segmentation as part of the planning process is to enable a firm to target its effort on the most promising opportunities. But what is an opportunity for firm A is not necessarily an opportunity for firm B. So a firm needs to develop a *typology* of the customer or segment it prefers, for this can be an instrument of great productivity in the market place.

The typology of the customer or the segment can be based on a myriad of criteria, as we have seen, such as:

Size of the firm
Its consumption level
Nature of its products/production/processes
Motivations of the decision-makers (e.g. desire to deal with big firms)
Geographical location, and so on

The whole point of segmentation is that a company must either:

Define its markets broadly enough to ensure that its costs for key activities are competitive; or

Define its markets in such a way that it can develop specialized skills in serving them to overcome a relative cost disadvantage.

Both have to be related to a firm's *distinctive competence* and to that of its competitors.

All of this should come to the fore as a result of the marketing audit referred to previously and should be summarized in the SWOT analysis. In particular, the differential benefits of a firm's product or service should be beyond doubt to all key members of the company.

To summarize, the objectives of market segmentation are:

To help determine marketing direction through the analysis and understanding of trends and buyer behaviour

To help determine realistic and obtainable marketing and sales objectives

To help improve decision-making by forcing managers to consider in depth the options ahead

Application questions

1 Choose a major product or service. Identify its features. Identify the benefits (to the customer) of each feature. Identify which of these benefits are differential benefits.

2 If you cannot identify any differential benefits, in what ways could you develop some?

3 For those you have identified, how can they be improved on?

4 Identify your key market segments. How do you describe them?

5 If you cannot identify any distinct segments, how can you begin to identify one or more?

5 Completing the Marketing Audit: 2
The Product Audit

What is a product?

The central role that the product plays in marketing management makes it such an important subject that mismanagement in this area is unlikely to be compensated for by good management in other areas.

The vital aspects of product management we shall discuss in this chapter are concerned with the nature of products, product life cycles, how products make profits, the concept of the product portfolio, and new product development. The purpose of this discussion is to help us to carry out a product audit in order that we can set meaningful marketing objectives. But before we can begin a proper discussion about product management, it is necessary first to understand what a product is, since this is the root of whatever misunderstanding there is about product management.

We have already looked at customers; now we begin to look at what we sell to them. Let us begin by explaining that a product is a problem solver, in the sense that it solves the customer's problems, and also is the means by which the company achieves its objectives. And since it is what actually changes hands, it is clearly a subject of great importance.

The clue to what constitutes a product can be found in an examination of what it is that customers appear to buy. For instance, Theodore Levitt, the famous management writer, illustrates that what customers want when they buy ¼ inch drills is ¼ inch holes. In other words the drill itself is only a means to an end. The lesson here for the drill manufacturer is that if he really believes his business is the manufacture of drills rather than, say, the manufacture of the means of making holes in materials, he is in grave danger of going out of business as soon as a better means of making holes is invented—such as, say, a pocket laser.

Figure 5.1

The important point about this is that a company which fails to think of its business in terms of customer benefits rather than in terms of physical products is in danger of losing its competitive position in the market.

But while this is important at the highest level of a company, it is also extremely relevant even at the level of the salesman. A salesman announcing that the quench tank on his furnace is three times bigger than the quench tank on that of his competitor must not be surprised if this news is met with complete indifference, especially if this feature requires a hole to be dug in the ground three times bigger than the one the customer currently has! Much more relevant would be the fact that this larger quench tank would enable the customer to save £10,000 a year on operating costs, which is a benefit and which is the main aspect the customer is interested in.

So far we have not mentioned service products, such as consulting, banking, insurance, and so on. The reason for this is simply that the marketing of services is not very different from the marketing of goods. The only difference is that a service product has benefits that cannot be stored. Thus, an airline seat, for example, if not utilized at the time of the flight, is gone forever, whereas a physical product may be stored and used at a later date.

In practice this disadvantage makes very little difference in marketing terms. The major problem seems to lie in the difficulty many service product companies have in actually perceiving and presenting their offerings as 'products'. Consider the example of the consultant. This country is full of a constantly changing army of people who set themselves up as consultants, and it is not unusual to see people presenting themselves, for example, as 'general marketing consultants'. It would be difficult for any prospective client to glean from such a description exactly what benefits this person is offering. Yet the market for consulting is no different from any other market, and it is a simple matter to segment the market and develop 'products' which will deliver the particular package of benefits desired.

We can now begin to see that when a customer buys a product, even if he is an industrial buyer purchasing a piece of equipment for his company, he is still buying a particular bundle of benefits which he perceives as satisfying his own particular needs and wants.

We can now begin to appreciate the danger of leaving product decisions entirely to engineers or R and D people. If we do, engineers will often assume that the only point in product management is the actual technical performance, or the functional features of the product itself.

These ideas are incorporated in Figure 5.2.

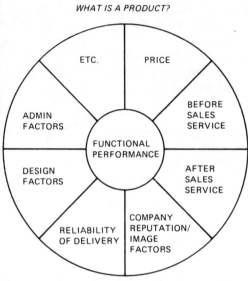

Figure 5.2

Product life cycle

Having discussed the vital factor of benefits as a part of product management, we must now ask ourselves whether one product is enough.

There are many examples of entrepreneurs who set themselves up in business to manufacture, say, toys such as clackers, who make their fortune and who then just as quickly lose it when this fashion-conscious market changes to its latest fad. Such examples are merely the extreme manifestation of what is known as the *product life cycle*. This too is such a vital and fundamental concept that it is worth devoting some time to a discussion of the subject.

Historians of technology have observed that all technical functions grow exponentially until they come up against some natural limiting factor which causes growth to slow down and eventually to decline as one technology is replaced by another. There is universal agreement that the same phenomenon applies to products, so giving rise to the concept of the product life cycle, much written about in marketing literature during the past three decades.

The product life cycle postulates that if a new product is successful at the introductory stage (and many fail at this point), then gradually repeat purchase grows and spreads and the rate of sales growth increases. At this stage competitors often enter the market and their additional promotional expenditures further expand the market. But no market is infinitely expandable, and eventually the *rate* of growth slows as the product moves into its maturity stage. Eventually a point is reached where there are too many firms in the market, price wars break out, and some firms drop out of the market, until finally the market itself eventually falls into decline. Figure 5.3 illustrates these apparently universal phenomena.

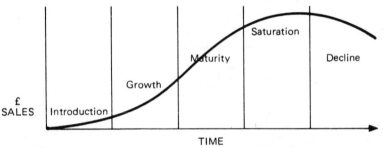

Figure 5.3

Nevertheless, while the product life cycle may well be a useful practical generalization, it can also be argued that particular product life cycles are determined more by the activities of the company than by any underlying 'law'. For example, a particular brand of cigarettes, while exhibiting all the characteristics of the classic product life cycle, went on to new record sales heights following the appointment of a new brand manager. Had this appointment not been made, the brand would probably have been withdrawn. Nevertheless, while this example illustrates the dangers inherent in incorrect interpretation of life cycle analysis, even in this case sales will eventually fall into decline as customer wants change.

From a management point of view, the product life cycle concept is useful in that it focuses our attention on the likely future sales pattern if we take no corrective action. There are several courses of action open to us in our attempts to maintain the profitable sales of a product over its life cycle. Figure 5.4 illustrates the actual courses taken by a British company in the management of one of its leading industrial market products. As sales growth began to slow down, the company initiated a programme of product range extensions and market development which successfully took the brand into additional stages of growth. At the same time the company was aggressively seeking new products and even considering potential areas for diversification.

Even more important are the implications of the product life cycle concept on every element of the marketing mix. The same diagram gives some guide as to how the product has to change over its life cycle. In addition to this, however, every other element also has to change. For example, if a company rigidly adhered to a premium pricing policy at the mature stage of the product life cycle, when markets are often overcrowded and price wars begin, it could well lose market share. It could be regretted later on when the market has settled down, for it is often at this stage that products provide extremely profitable revenue for the company. It will become clearer later in this chapter why market share is important.

The same applies to promotion. During the early phase of product introduction, the task for advertising is usually one of creating awareness, whereas during the growth phase the task is likely to change to one of creating a favourable attitude towards the product. Neither should the policy towards channels be fixed. At first we are concerned with getting distribution for the product in the most important channels, whereas during the growth phase we have to consider ways of reaching the new channels that want our product. All of these points will become clearer in those chapters specifically concerned with the management of price, place and promotion.

Drawing a product life cycle can be extremely difficult, even given the availability of some form of time series analysis. This is connected with the complex question of market share measurement.

Firstly, let us remind ourselves that a firm needs to be concerned with its share (or its proportion of volume or value) of an *actual* market rather than with a *potential* market. The example of the carpet manufacturer given in Chapter 4 emphasized the importance of measuring the right things when determining what a company's market is.

For the purpose of helping us to draw life cycles, it is worth repeating the definitions given in Chapter 3:

> Product class, e.g. carpets
> Product form, e.g. nylon rolls
> Product brand, e.g. 'X'

'X' as a brand, for the purpose of measuring market share, is *concerned only with the aggregate of all other brands that satisfy the same group of customer wants.*

Nevertheless, the manufacturer of 'X' also needs to be aware of the sales trends of other kinds of carpets and floor covering in the institutional market, as well as of carpet sales overall.

One of the most frequent mistakes made by companies that do not understand what market share really means, is to assume that their company has only a small share of some market, whereas if the company is commer-

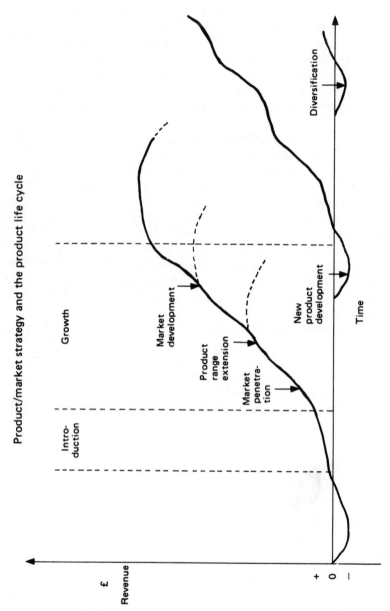

Figure 5.4

cially successful, it probably has a much larger share of a smaller market segment.

The important point to remember at this stage is that the concept of the product life cycle is not an academic figment of the imagination, but a hard reality which is ignored at great risk. It is interesting to see how many commercial failures can be traced back to a naive assumption on the part of managements that what was successful as a policy at one time will continue to be successful in the future.

Table 5.1 shows a checklist used by one major company to help it determine where its markets are on the life cycle.

Product portfolio

We might well imagine that at any point in time a review of a company's different products would reveal different stages of growth, maturity and decline.

In Figure 5.5, the dotted line represents the time of our analysis, and this shows one product in severe decline, one product in its introductory stage, and one in the saturation stage.

If our objective is to grow in profitability over a long period of time, our analysis of our product portfolio should reveal a situation like the one in Figure 5.6, in which new product introductions are timed so as to ensure continuous sales growth.

The idea of a portfolio is for a company to meet its objectives by balancing sales growth, cash flow, and risk. As individual products progress or decline and as markets grow or shrink, then the overall nature of the company's product portfolio will change. It is therefore essential that the whole portfolio is reviewed regularly and that an active policy towards new product development and divestment of old products is pursued. In this respect, the work of the Boston Consulting Group over the past decade has had a profound effect on the way managements think about this subject and about their product/market strategy.

Unit costs and market share

There are basically two parts to the thinking behind the work of the Boston Consulting Group. One is concerned with *market share*; the other with *market growth*.

It is a well-known fact that we become better at doing things the more we do them. This phenomenon is known as the *learning curve*. It manifests itself especially with items such as labour efficiency, work specialization, and methods improvement.

Table 5.1 Guide to market maturity

Maturity stage Factor	Embryonic	Growth	Mature	Declining
1 *Growth rate*	Normally much greater than GNP (on small base).	Sustained growth above GNP. New customers. New suppliers. Rate decelerates toward end of stage.	Approximately equals GNP.	Declining demand. Market shrinks as users' needs change.
2 *Predictability of growth potential*	Hard to define accurately. Small portion of demand being satisfied. Market forecasts differ widely.	Greater percentage of demand is met and upper limits of demand becoming clearer. Discontinuities, such as price reductions based on economies of scale, may occur.	Potential well defined. Competition specialized to satisfy needs of specific segments.	Known and limited.
3 *Product line proliferation*	Specialized lines to meet needs of early customers.	Rapid expansion.	Proliferation slows or ceases.	Lines narrow as unprofitable products dropped.
4 *Number of competitors*	Unpredictable.	Reaches maximum. New entrants attracted by growth and high margins. Some consolidation begins toward end of stage.	Entrenched positions established. Further shakeout of marginal competitors.	New entrants unlikely. Competitors continue to decline.
5 *Market share distribution*	Unstable. Shares react unpredictably to entrepreneurial insights and timing.	Increasing stability. Typically, a few competitors emerging as strong.	Stable with a few companies often controlling much of industry.	Highly concentrated or fragmented as industry segments and/or is localized.

Table 5.1 – *cont.*

6	*Customer stability*	Trial usage with little customer loyalty.	Some loyalty. Repeat usage with many seeking alternative suppliers.	Well-developed buying patterns with customer loyalty. Competitors understand purchase dynamics and it is difficult for a new supplier to win over accounts.	Extremely stable. Suppliers dwindle and customers less motivated to seek alternatives.
7	*Ease of entry*	Normally easy. No one dominates. Customers' expectations uncertain. If barriers exist, they are usually technology, capital or fear of the unknown.	More difficult. Market franchises and/or economies of scale may exist, yet new business is still available without directly confronting competition.	Difficult. Market leaders established. New business must be 'won' from others.	Little or no incentive to enter.
8	*Technology*	Plays an important role in matching product characteristics to market needs. Frequent product changes.	Product technology vital early, while process technology more important later in this stage.	Process and material substitution focus. Product requirements well known and relatively undemanding. May be a thrust to renew the industry via new technology.	Technological content is known, stable and accessible.

Such benefits are themselves a part of what we can call the *experience effect*, which includes such items as process innovations, better productivity from plant and equipment, product design improvements, and so on. In addition to the experience effect, and not necessarily mutually exclusive, are *economies of scale* that come with growth. For example, capital costs do not increase in direct proportion to capacity, which results in lower depreciation charges per unit of output, lower operating costs in the form of the number of operatives, lower marketing, sales, administration, and research and development costs, and lower raw materials and shipping costs.

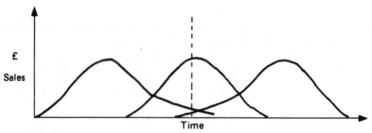

Figure 5.5

There is an overwhelming body of evidence to show that this is so, in which case it follows that the greater your volume, the lower your unit costs should be. Thus, irrespective of what happens to the price of your product, providing you have the highest market share (hence the biggest volume), you should always be relatively more profitable than your competitors. This is illustrated in Figure 5.7.

Thus, as a general rule, it can be said that market share *per se* is a desirable goal. However, as we made clear in Chapter 4, we have to be certain that we have carefully defined our market, or segment. This explains why it is apparently possible for many small firms to be profitable in large markets. The reason is, of course, that in reality they have a large share of a smaller market segment. This is another reason why understanding market segmentation is the key to successful marketing. It would be unusual if there were not many caveats to the above 'law', and, although what these might be are fairly obvious, nevertheless it should be noted that the evidence provided by the Boston Consulting Group shows overwhelmingly that in general these 'laws' apply universally, whether for consumer, industrial or service markets.

Turning now to *market growth*, we observe that in markets which are growing at a very low rate per annum, it is extremely difficult and also very costly, to increase your market share. This is usually because the market is in the steady state (possibly in the saturation phase of the product life cycle)

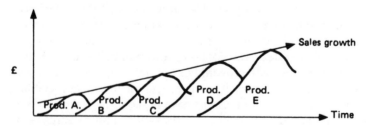

Figure 5.6

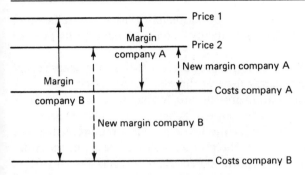

Figure 5.7

and is dominated by a few major firms who have probably reached a stage of equilibrium, which it is very difficult to upset.

In markets which are going through a period of high growth, it is fairly obvious that the most sensible policy to pursue would be to gain market share by taking a bigger proportion of the market growth than your competitors. However, such a policy is very costly in promotional terms. So many companies prefer to sit tight and enjoy rates of growth lower than the market rate. The major problem with this approach is that they are in fact losing market share, which gives cost advantages (hence margin advantages) to competitors.

Since we know from previous experience of product life cycles that the market growth rate will fall, when this stage is reached and the market inevitably becomes price sensitive, the product will begin to lose money and we will probably be forced out of the market. Indeed, seen in this light, it becomes easier to understand the reasons for the demise. of many British industries, such as the motor-cycle industry, in which the output of the Japanese increased from thousands of units to millions of units during a period of market growth, while the output of the British remained steady during the same period. When the market growth rate started to decline, the inevitable happened. Even worse, it is virtually impossible to recover from such a situation, while the Japanese, with their advantageous cost position, have now dominated practically every market segment including big bikes.

The Boston matrix

The Boston Consulting Group combined these ideas in the form of a simple matrix, which has profound implications for the firm, especially in respect of *cash flow*. Profits are not always an appropriate indicator of portfolio performance, as they will often reflect changes in the liquid assets of the company such as inventories, capital equipment, or receivables, and thus do not indicate the true scope for future development. Cash flow, on the other hand, is a key determinant of a company's ability to develop its product portfolio.

The Boston matrix classifies a firm's products according to their cash usage and their cash generation along the two dimensions described above, i.e. relative market share and market growth rate. Market share is used because it is an indicator of the product's ability to generate cash; market growth is used because it is an indicator of the product's cash requirements. The measure of market share used is the product's share *relative* to the firm's largest competitor. This is important because it reflects the degree of dominance enjoyed by the product in the market. For example, if company A has 20 per cent market share and its biggest competitor also has 20 per cent market share, this position is usually less favourable than if company A had 20 per cent market share and its biggest competitor had only 10 per cent market share. The relative ratios would be 1:1 compared with 2:1. It is this ratio, or measure of market dominance, that the horizontal axis measures. This is summarized in Figure 5.8.

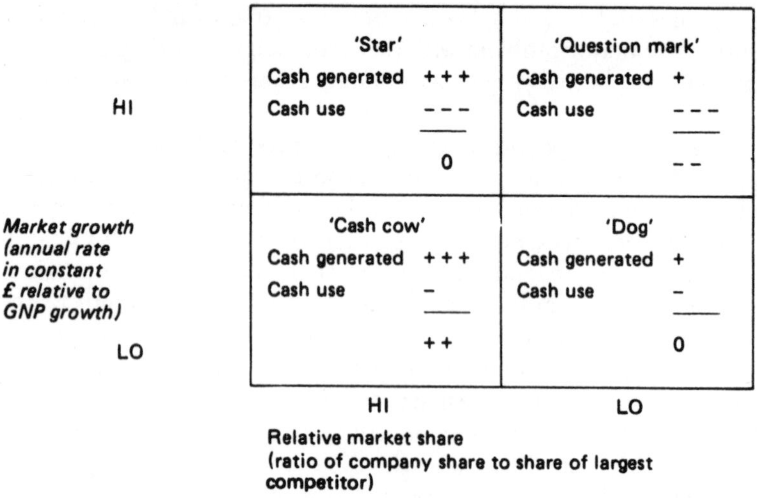

	'Star'	'Question mark'
HI	Cash generated + + + Cash use – – – 0	Cash generated + Cash use – – – – –
Market growth (annual rate in constant £ relative to GNP growth) **LO**	'Cash cow' Cash generated + + + Cash use – ──── + +	'Dog' Cash generated + Cash use – ──── 0
	HI	LO

Relative market share
(ratio of company share to share of largest
competitor)

Figure 5.8

The definition of high relative market share is taken to be a ratio of one or more. The cut-off point for high as opposed to low market growth should be defined according to the prevailing circumstances in the industry, but this is often taken as 10 per cent.

The somewhat picturesque labels attached to each of the four categories of products give some indication of the prospects for products in each quadrant. Thus, the 'question mark' is a product which has not yet achieved a dominant market position and thus a high cash flow, or perhaps it once had such a position but has slipped back. It will be a high user of cash because it is in a growth market. This is also sometimes referred to as a 'wildcat'.

The 'star' is probably a newish product that has achieved a high market share and which is probably more or less self-financing in cash terms.

The 'cash cows' are leaders in markets where there is little additional growth, but a lot of stability. These are excellent generators of cash and tend to use little because of the state of the market.

'Dogs' have little future and are often a cash drain on the company. They are probably candidates for divestment, although often such products fall into a category aptly described by Peter Drucker as 'investments in managerial ego'.

The art of product portfolio management now becomes a lot clearer. What we should be seeking to do is to use the surplus cash generated by the 'cash cows' to invest in our 'stars' and to invest in a selected number of 'question marks'. This is indicated in Figure 5.9.

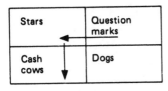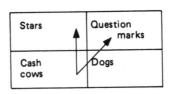

1. Ideal product development sequence   2.   Internal flow of funds

Figure 5.9

The Boston matrix can be used to forecast the market position of our products, say, five years from now if we continue to pursue our current policies. Figure 5.10 illustrates this process for a manufacturer of plastic valves. The area of each circle is proportional to each product's contribution

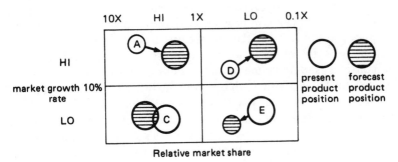

Figure 5.10

to total company sales volume. In the case of this particular company, it can be seen that they are following what could well prove to be disastrous policies in respect of their principal products.

Such a framework also easily helps to explain the impracticability of marketing objectives such as 'to achieve a 10 per cent growth and a 20 per cent return on investment'. Such an objective, while fine as an *overall* policy, if applied to individual products in the portfolio, clearly becomes a nonsense and totally self-defeating. For example, to accept a 10 per cent growth rate in a market which is growing at, say, 15 per cent per annum, is likely to prove disastrous in the long run. Likewise, to go for a much higher than market growth rate in a low-growth market is certain to lead to unnecessary price wars and market disruption.

This type of framework is particularly useful to demonstrate to senior management the implications of different product/market strategies. It is also useful in formulating policies towards new product development.

Other key uses of the Boston matrix

One of the key assumptions of the Boston matrix is that margins and cash generated depend on high relative market share. One other not directly related to the work of the Boston Consulting Group but compatible with it is that market share and profitability are linearly related.

Unfortunately, all of this depends on how 'market' is defined in measuring market share. Also, market share for some products may have little relationship with profitability. For example, the profitability of chemical products may have very little to do with their relative market shares, since profitability may be determined by some composite production process through which they all pass at an early stage in manufacture. Other areas of the business which may be key in the accumulation of experience could include: the provision of raw materials; component production; assembly; distribution; selling; advertising and promotion; and so on.

It is such complications that make the Boston matrix less relevant to certain situations. While it is impossible to give absolute rules on what these situations are, suffice it to say that great caution is necessary when dealing with such matters. In any case, two principles should be adhered to always. Firstly, a business should define its markets in such a way that it can ensure that its costs for key activities will be competitive. Or, it should define the markets it serves in such a way that it can develop specialized skills in servicing those markets and hence overcome a relative cost disadvantage. Both, of course, have to be related to a company's *distinctive competence*.

However, the approach of the Boston Consulting Group is fairly criticized in such circumstances as those described above as relying on two single factors. To overcome this difficulty, General Electric and McKinsey jointly developed a multi-factor approach using the same fundamental ideas as the Boston Consulting Group. They used *industry attractiveness* and *business strengths* as the two main axes and built up these dimensions from a number of variables. Using these variables, and some scheme for weighting them according to their importance, products (or businesses) are classified into one of nine cells in a 3 × 3 matrix. Thus, the same purpose is served as in the Boston matrix (i.e. comparing investment opportunities among products or businesses) but with the difference that multiple criteria are used. These criteria vary according to circumstances, but generally include those shown in Figure 5.11.

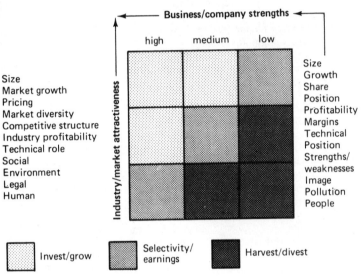

Figure 5.11

Whichever approach is used, it can be seen that obvious consideration should be given towards marketing objectives and strategies which are appropriate to the attractiveness of a market (market growth in Boston matrix) and the extent to which such opportunities match our capabilities (market share in Boston matrix). The general guidelines which are given in Table 5.2 and Figure 5.12 can be applied to either the four-box or the nine-box matrix equally well.

One final word of warning is necessary. Such general guidelines should not be followed unquestioningly. They are intended more as checklists of questions that should be asked about each major product in each major market *before* setting marketing objectives and strategies.

Table 5.2 Strategies suggested by portfolio matrix analysis

	Relative market share (or business strengths)	
	High	**Low**
High **Relative market growth** (%) 10 (or market attractiveness)	*Invest for growth* Defend leadership, gain if possible Accept moderate short-term profits and negative cash flow Consider geographic expansion, product line expansion, product differentiation Upgrade product introduction effort Aggressive marketing posture, viz. selling, advertising, pricing, sales promotion, service levels, as appropriate	*Opportunistic development* Invest heavily in selective products As for 'Invest for growth'

	Maintain market position, manage for earnings	*'Cash dogs'*	Genuine *'dogs'*
Low	Maintain market position in most successful product lines Prune less successful product lines Differentiate products to maintain share of key segments Limit discretionary marketing expenditure Stabilize prices, except where a temporary aggressive stance is necessary to maintain market share	Acknowledge low growth Do not view as a 'marketing' problem Identify and exploit growth segments Emphasize product quality to avoid 'commodity' competition Systematically improve productivity Assign talented managers	Prune product line aggressively Maximize cash flow Minimize marketing expenditure Maintain or raise prices at the expense of volume

0

10.0   1.0   0.1

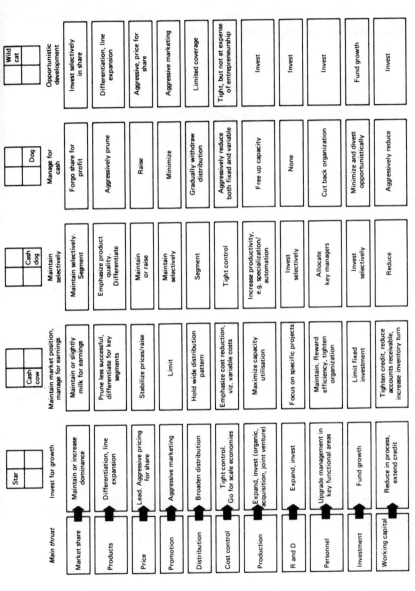

The matrix shows the following functional guidelines across the positions Star, Cash cow, Cash dog, Dog, and Wild cat:

Main thrust	Star: Invest for growth	Cash cow: Maintain market position, manage for earnings	Cash dog: Maintain selectively	Dog: Manage for cash	Wild cat: Opportunistic development
Market share	Maintain or increase dominance	Maintain or slightly milk for earnings	Maintain selectively. Segment	Forgo share for profit	Invest selectively in share
Products	Differentiation, line expansion	Prune less successful, differentiate for key segments	Emphasize product quality. Differentiate	Aggressively prune	Differentiation, line expansion
Price	Lead. Aggressive pricing for share	Stabilize prices/raise	Maintain or raise	Raise	Aggressive, price for share
Promotion	Aggressive marketing	Limit	Maintain selectively	Minimize	Aggressive marketing
Distribution	Broaden distribution	Hold wide distribution pattern	Segment	Gradually withdraw distribution	Limited coverage
Cost control	Tight control. Go for scale economies	Emphasize cost reduction, viz. variable costs	Tight control	Aggressively reduce both fixed and variable	Tight, but not at expense of entrepreneurship
Production	Expand, invest (organic, acquisition, joint venture)	Maximize capacity utilisation	Increase productivity, e.g. specialization/automation	Free up capacity	Invest
R and D	Expand, invest	Focus on specific projects	Invest selectively	None	Invest
Personnel	Upgrade management in key functional areas	Maintain. Reward efficiency, tighten organization	Allocate key managers	Cut back organization	Invest
Investment	Fund growth	Limit fixed investment	Invest selectively	Minimize and divest opportunistically	Fund growth
Working capital	Reduce in process, extend credit	Tighten credit, reduce accounts receivable, increase inventory turn	Reduce	Aggressively reduce	Invest

Figure 5.12 Other functional guidelines suggested by portfolio matrix analysis.

Combining product life cycles and portfolio management

Figure 5.13 illustrates the consequences of failing to appreciate the implications of both the product life cycle concept and the dual combination of market share and market growth.

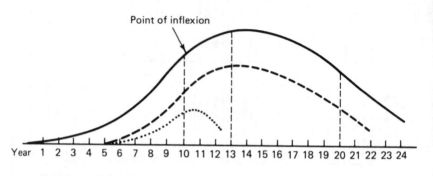

Figure 5.13 Short-term profit maximization versus market share and long-term profit maximization.

Companies A and B both start out with question marks (wildcats) in years 5 and 6 in a growing market. Company A invests in building market share and quickly turns the product into a star. Company B, meanwhile, manages its product for profit over a four-year period so that, while still growing, it steadily loses market share (i.e. it remains a question mark or wildcat).

In year 10, when the market becomes saturated (when typically competitive pressures intensify), Company B with its low market share (hence typically higher costs and lower margins) cannot compete and quickly drops out of the market. Company A, on the other hand, aggressively defends its market share and goes on to enjoy a period of approximately ten years with a product which has become a cash cow. Thus, Company B, by pursuing a policy of short-term profit maximization, lost at least ten years profit potential.

Relevance of life-cycle analysis and portfolio management to the marketing audit

It will be recalled that this discussion took place against the background of the need to complete a full and detailed marketing audit prior to setting marketing objectives. While such analyses as those described in this chapter should be an integral part of the marketing audit, life cycles and portfolio matrices should also appear in the SWOT analysis.

The SWOT analysis should contain a product life cycle for each major product and an attempt should be made (using the audit information) to predict the future shape of the life cycle. It should also contain a product portfolio matrix showing the present position of the products and the future desired position of the same products (e.g. for five years ahead, if this is the planning horizon). The matrix may therefore have to include some products not currently in the range.

Application questions

1 Select a major product and draw a life cycle of:
   —the product itself;
   —the market (segment) in which it competes.
2 Explain why it is the shape it is.
3 Predict the shape and length of the life cycle in the future.
4 Say *why* you are making these predictions.
5 Plot your products on a Boston matrix.
6 Explain their relative positions.
7 Forecast where they will be (and why), say, five years from now.

6 Setting Marketing Objectives and Strategies

Without doubt, this is the key step in the marketing planning process, for it will by now be clear that following the analysis that takes place as part of the marketing audit, realistic and achievable objectives should be set for the company's major products in each of its major markets. Unless this step is carried out well, everything that follows will lack focus and cohesion. It is really a question of deciding on the right target. After all, it is no good scoring a bulls-eye on the wrong target!

Marketing objectives: what they are and how they relate to corporate objectives

There are no works on marketing which do not include at least one paragraph on the need for setting objectives. Setting objectives is a mandatory step in the planning process. The literature on the subject though is not very explicit, which is surprising when it is considered how vital the setting of marketing objectives is.

An objective will ensure that a company knows what its strategies are expected to accomplish and when a particular strategy has accomplished its purpose. In other words, without objectives, strategy decisions and all that follows will take place in a vacuum.

Following the identification of opportunities and the explicit statement of assumptions about conditions affecting the business, the process of setting objectives in theory should be comparatively easy, the actual objectives themselves being a realistic statement of what the company desires to achieve as a result of a market-centred analysis, rather than generalized statements born of top management's desire to 'do better next year'. However, objective setting is more complex than at first it would appear to be.

82

Most experts agree that the logical approach to the difficult task of setting marketing objectives is to proceed from the broad to the specific. Thus, the starting point would be a statement of the nature of the business, from which would flow the broad company objectives. Next, the broad company objectives would be translated into key result areas, which would be those areas in which success is vital to the firm. Market penetration, and growth rate of sales, are examples of key result areas. The third step would be creation of the sub-objectives necessary to accomplish the broad objectives, such as sales volume goals, geographical expansion, product line extension, and so on.

The end result of this process should be objectives which are consistent with the strategic plan, attainable within budget limitations, and compatible with the strengths, limitations, and economics of other functions within the organization.

At the top level, management is concerned with long-run profitability; at the next level in the management hierarchy, the concern is for objectives which are defined more specifically and in greater detail, such as increasing sales and market share, obtaining new markets, and so on. These objectives are merely a part of the hierarchy of objectives, in that corporate objectives will only be accomplished if these and other objectives are achieved. At the next level, management is concerned with objectives which are defined even more tightly, such as: to create awareness among a specific target market about a new product; to change a particular customer attitude; and so on. Again, the general marketing objectives will only be accomplished if these and other sub-objectives are achieved. It is clear that sub-objectives *per se*, unless they are an integral part of a broader framework of objectives, are likely to lead to a wasteful misdirection of resources.

For example, a sales increase in itself may be possible, but only at an undue cost, so that such a marketing objective is only appropriate within the framework of corporate objectives. In such a case, it may well be that an increase in sales in a particular market sector will entail additional capital expenditure ahead of the time for which it is planned. If this were the case, it may make more sense to allocate available production capacity to more profitable market sectors in the short term, allowing sales to decline in another sector. Decisions such as this are likely to be more easily made against a backcloth of explicitly stated broad company objectives relating to all the major disciplines.

Likewise, objectives should be set for advertising, for example, which are wholly consistent with wider objectives. Objectives set in this way integrate the advertising effort with the other elements in the marketing mix and this leads to a consistent, logical marketing plan.

So what is a corporate objective and what is a marketing objective?

A business starts at some time with resources and wants to use those resources to achieve something. What the business wants to achieve is a corporate objective, which describes a desired destination, or result. How it is to be achieved is a strategy. In a sense, this means that the only true objective of a company is, by definition, what is stated in the corporate plan as being the principal purpose of its existence. Most often this is expressed in terms of profit, since profit is the means of satisfying shareholders or owners, and because it is the one universally accepted criterion by which efficiency can be evaluated, which will in turn lead to efficient resource allocation, economic and technological progressiveness and stability.

This means that stated desires, such as to expand market share, to create a new image, to achieve an x per cent increase in sales, and so on, are in fact strategies at the corporate level, since they are the means by which a company will achieve its profit objectives. In practice, however, companies tend to operate by means of functional divisions, each with a separate identity, so that what is a strategy in the corporate plan becomes an objective within each department. For example, marketing strategies within the corporate plan become operating objectives within the marketing department and strategies at the general level within the marketing department themselves become operating objectives at the next level down, so that an intricate web of inter-related objectives and strategies is built up at all levels within the framework of the overall company plan.

The really important point, however, apart from clarifying the difference between objectives and strategies, is that the further down the hierarchical chain one goes, the less likely it is that a stated objective will make a cost-effective contribution to company profits, unless it derives logically and directly from an objective at a higher level.

Corporate objectives and strategies can be simplified in the following way:

Corporate objective   — desired level of profitability
Corporate strategies — which products and which markets (marketing)
                        — what kind of facilities (production and distribution)
                        — size and character of the staff/labour force (personnel)
                        — funding (finance)
                        — other corporate strategies such as social responsibility, corporate image, stock market image, employee image, etc.

It is now clear that at the next level down in the organization, i.e. functional level, what products are to be sold into what markets, become *marketing objectives*, while the means of achieving these objectives using the marketing mix, are *marketing strategies*. At the next level down there would be, say, *advertising objectives* and *advertising strategies*, with the subsequent *programmes* and *budgets* for achieving the objectives. In this way, a hierarchy of objectives and strategies can be traced back to the initial corporate objective. Figure 6.1 illustrates this point.

How to set marketing objectives

In Chapter 2 the Ansoff matrix was introduced as a useful tool for thinking about marketing objectives.

A firm's competitive situation can be simplified to two dimensions only—products and markets. To put it even more simply, Ansoff's framework is about what is sold (the 'product'), and who it is sold to (the 'market'). Within this framework Ansoff identifies four possible courses of action for the firm:

Selling existing products to existing markets
Extending existing products to new markets
Developing new products for existing markets
Developing new products for new markets

The matrix in Figure 6.2 depicts these concepts.

It is clear that the range of possible marketing objectives is very wide, since there will be degrees of technological newness and degrees of market newness. Nevertheless, Ansoff's matrix provides a logical framework in which marketing objectives can be developed under each of the four main headings above. *In other words, marketing objectives are about products and markets only*. Commonsense will confirm that it is only by selling something to someone that the company's financial goals can be achieved, and that advertising, pricing, service levels, and so on, are the means (or strategies) by which it might succeed in doing this. Thus, pricing objectives, sales promotion objectives, advertising objectives, and the like should not be confused with marketing objectives.

Marketing objectives are generally accepted as being selected qualitative and quantitative commitments, usually stated either in standards of performance for a given operating period, or conditions to be achieved by given dates. Performance standards are usually stated in terms of sales volume and various measures of profitability. The conditions to be attained are usually a percentage of market share and various other commitments, such as a percentage of the total number of a given type of retail outlet.

There is also broad agreement that objectives must be specific enough to

Marketing planning in a
corporate framework

Corporate mission

Define the business and its boundaries
using considerations such as:
— distinctive competence
— environmental trends
— consumption market trends
— resource market trends
— stakeholder expectations

Corporate objectives

e.g. ROI, ROSHF, image (with stock market, public and employees), social responsibility, etc.

Corporate strategies

e.g. involve corporate resources, and must be within corporate business boundaries

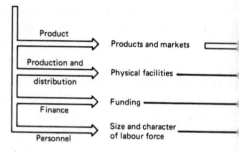

Product

Products and markets

Production and

distribution

Physical facilities

Finance

Funding

Personnel

Size and character
of labour force

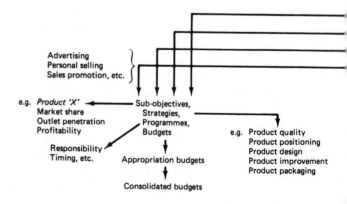

Advertising
Personal selling
Sales promotion, etc.

e.g. *Product 'X'*
Market share
Outlet penetration
Profitability

Responsibility
Timing, etc.

Sub-objectives,
Strategies,
Programmes,
Budgets

Appropriation budgets

Consolidated budgets

e.g. Product quality
Product positioning
Product design
Product improvement
Product packaging

Figure 6.1

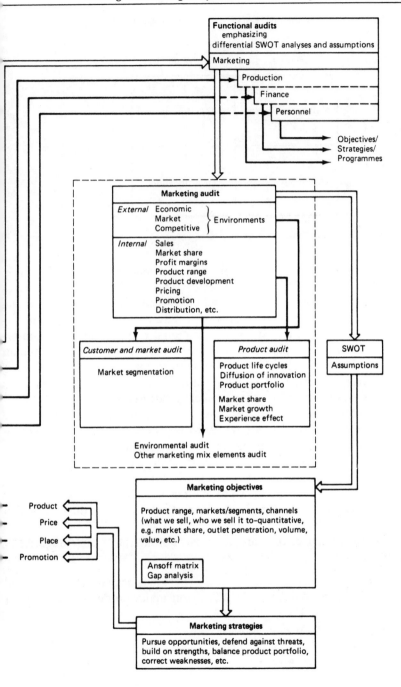

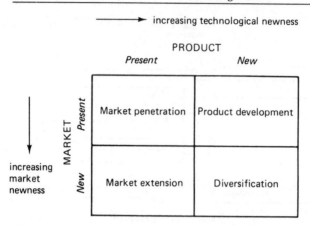

Figure 6.2   Ansoff matrix.

enable subordinates to derive from them the general character of action required and the yardstick by which performance is to be judged. Objectives are the core of managerial action, providing direction to the plans. By asking where the operation should be at some future date, objectives are determined. Vague objectives, however emotionally appealing, are counterproductive to sensible planning, and are usually the result of the human propensity for wishful thinking which often smacks more of cheerleading than serious marketing leadership. What this really means is that while it is arguable whether directional terms such as 'decrease', 'optimize', 'minimize' should be used as objectives, it seems logical that unless there is some measure, or yardstick, against which to measure a sense of locomotion towards achieving them, then they do not serve any useful purpose.

Ansoff defines an objective as 'a measure of the efficiency of the resource-conversion process. An objective contains three elements: the particular attribute that is chosen as a measure of efficiency; the yardstick or scale by which the attribute is measured; and the particular value on the scale which the firm seeks to attain'.

Marketing objectives then are about each of the four main categories of the Ansoff matrix:

1   *Existing products in existing markets.* These may be many and varied and will certainly need to be set for all existing major products and customer groups (segments).
2   *New products in existing markets.*
3   *Existing products in new markets.*
4   *New products in new markets.*

Thus, in the long run, it is only by selling something (a 'product') to someone (a 'market') that any firm can succeed in staying in business profitably. Simply defined, product/market strategy means the route chosen to achieve company goals through the range of products it offers to its chosen market segments. Thus the product/market strategy represents a commitment to a future direction for the firm. Marketing objectives, then, are concerned solely with products and markets.

The general marketing *directions* which lead to the above objectives flow of course from the life cycle and portfolio analysis conducted in the audit and revolve around the following logical decisions:

1 *Maintain*. This usually refers to the 'cash cow' type of product/market and reflects the desire to maintain competitive positions.
2 *Improve*. This usually refers to the 'star' type of products/market and reflects the desire to improve the competitive position in attractive markets.
3 *Harvest*. This usually refers to the 'dog' type of product/market and reflects the desire to relinquish competitive position in favour of short-term profit and cash flow.
4 *Exit*. This also usually refers to the 'dog' type of product/market, also sometimes the 'wildcat', and reflects a desire to divest because of a weak competitive position or because the cost of staying in it is prohibitive and the risk associated with improving its position is too high.
5 *Enter*. This usually refers to a new business area.

As already stated, however, great care should be taken not to follow slavishly any set of 'rules' or guidelines related to the above. Also, the use of pejorative labels like 'dog', 'cash cow', and so on should be avoided if possible.

Figure 6.3 illustrates what is commonly referred to as 'gap analysis'. Essentially what it says is that if the corporate sales and financial objectives are greater than the current long-range forecasts, there is a gap which has to be filled.

The 'operations gap' can be filled in two ways:

1 Improved productivity, e.g. reduce costs, improve the sales mix, increase prices.
2 Market penetration, e.g. increase usage, increase market share.

The 'new strategies gap' can be filled in four ways:

1 Reduce objectives.
2 Market extension, e.g. find new user groups, enter new segments, geographical expansion.

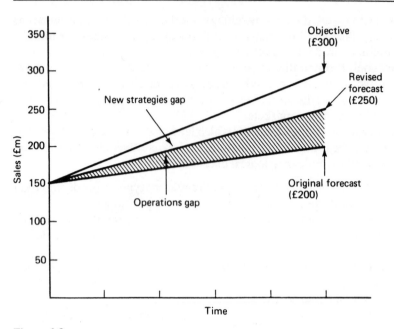

Figure 6.3

3 Product development.
4 Diversification, e.g. selling new products to new markets.

If improved productivity is one method by which the expansion gap is to be filled, care must be taken not to take measures such as to reduce marketing costs by 20 per cent overall. The portfolio analysis undertaken during the marketing audit stage will indicate that this would be totally inappropriate to some product/market areas, for which increased marketing expenditure may be needed, while for others 20 per cent reduction in marketing costs may not be sufficient.

As for the other options, it is clear that market penetration should always be a company's first option, since it makes far more sense to attempt to increase profits and cash flow from *existing* products and markets initially, because this is usually the least costly and the least risky. This is so because for its present products and markets a company has developed knowledge and skills which it can use competitively.

For the same reason, it makes more sense in many cases to move along the horizontal axis for further growth before attempting to find new markets. The reason for this is that it normally takes many years for a company to get to know its customers and markets and to build up a reputation. That reputation and trust embodied in either the company's name or in its brands, is rarely transferable to new markets, where other companies are already entrenched.

The marketing audit should ensure that the method chosen to fill the gap is consistent with the company's capabilities and builds on its strengths. For example, it would normally prove far less profitable for a dry goods grocery manufacturer to introduce frozen foods than to add another dry foods product. Likewise, if a product could be sold to existing channels using the existing sales force, this is far less risky than introducing a new product that requires new channels and new selling skills.

Exactly the same applies to the company's production, distribution, and people. Whatever new products are developed should be as consistent as possible with the company's known strengths and capabilities. Clearly, the use of existing plant capacity is generally preferable to new processes. Also, the amount of additional investment is important. Technical personnel are highly trained and specialist, and whether this competence can be transferred to a new field must be considered. A product requiring new raw materials may also require new handling and storage techniques which may prove expensive.

It can now be appreciated why going into new markets with new products (diversification) is the riskiest strategy of all, because *new* resources and *new* management skills have to be developed. This is why the history of commerce is replete with examples of companies which went bankrupt through moving into areas where they had little or no distinctive competence. This is also why many companies that diversified through acquisition during periods of high economic growth have since divested themselves of businesses that were not basically compatible with their own distinctive competence.

The Ansoff matrix, of course, is not a simple four-box matrix for it will be obvious that there are degrees of technological newness as well as degrees of market newness. Figure 6.4 illustrates the point. It also demonstrates more easily why any movement should generally aim to keep a company as close as possible to its present position rather than moving it to a totally unrelated position, except in the most unusual circumstances.

Nevertheless, the product life cycle phenomenon will inevitably *force* companies to move along one or more of the Ansoff matrix axes if they are to continue to increase their sales and profits. A key question to be asked then is *how* this important decision is to be taken, given the risks involved.

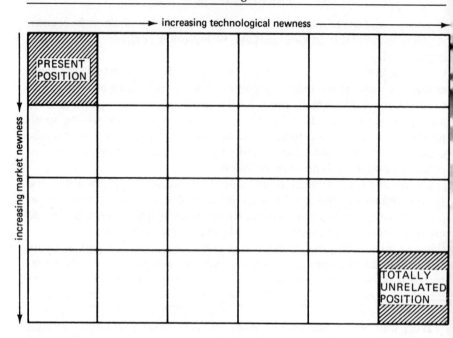

Figure 6.4

New product development/market extension/diversification

The answer, of course, should be comparatively simple if the marketing audit has been completed thoroughly.

It is not the purpose here to explore in detail sub-sets of marketing, such as market research, market selection, new product development, and diversification. What is important, however, in a book on marketing planning is to communicate an understanding of the framework in which these activities should take place.

What we are aiming to do is to maximize *synergy*, which could be described as the 2 + 2 = 5 effect. The starting point is the marketing audit, leading to the SWOT (strengths, weaknesses, opportunities and threats) analysis. This is so that development of any kind will be firmly based within a company's basic *strengths* and *weaknesses*. External factors are the opportunities and threats facing the company.

Once this important analytical stage is successfully completed, the more technical process of opportunity identification, screening, business analysis, and finally activities such as product development, testing and entry planning can take place depending on which option is selected. The important point to remember is that no matter how thoroughly these subsequent activities are carried out, unless the objectives of product development/ market extension are based firmly on an analysis of the company's capabilities, they are unlikely to be successful in the long term. Figure 6.5 illustrates the process.

The criteria selected will generally be consistent with the criteria used for positioning products or businesses in the nine-cell portfolio matrix described in Chapter 5. The list shown in Table 6.1, however, (which is also totally consistent with the marketing audit checklist) can be used to select those criteria which are most important. A rating and weighting system can then be applied to opportunities identified to assess their suitability or otherwise. Those criteria selected and the weighting system used will, of course, be consistent with the SWOT analysis.

A simple example is given in Table 6.2 of a quantitative approach to evaluation once the criteria have been selected.

Marketing strategies

What a company wants to accomplish, then, in terms of such things as market share and volume, is a marketing objective. How the company

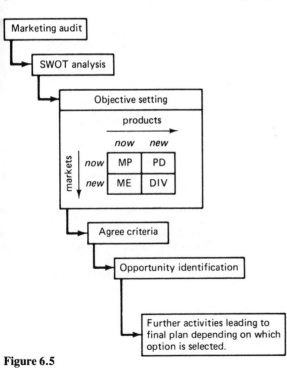

Figure 6.5

Table 6.1   Factors contributing to market attractiveness and business position

Attractiveness of your market	*Status/position of your business*
Market factors	
Size (money units or both)	Your share (in equivalent terms)
Size of key segments	Your share of key segments
Growth rate per year:	Your annual growth rate:
total	total
segments	segments
Diversity of market	Diversity of your participation
Sensitivity to price, service features and external factors	Your influence on the market
Cyclicality	Lags or leads in your sales
Seasonality	
Bargaining power of upstream suppliers	Bargaining power of your suppliers
Bargaining power of downstream suppliers	Bargaining power of your customers
Competition	Where you fit, how you compare in
Types of competitors	terms of products, marketing capability,
Degree of concentration	service, production strength, financial
Changes in type and mix	strength, management
Entries and exits	Segments you have entered or left
Changes in share	Your relative share change
Substitution by new technology	Your vulnerability to new technology
Degrees and types of integration	Your own level of integration
Financial and economic factors	
Contribution margins	Your margins
Leveraging factors, such as economies of scale and experience	Your scale and experience
Barriers to entry or exit (both financial and non-financial)	Barriers to your entry or exit (both financial and non-financial)
Capacity utilization	Your capacity utilization
Technological factors	
Maturity and volatility	Your ability to cope with change
Complexity	Depths of your skills
Differentiation	Types of your technological skills
Patents and copyrights	Your patent protection
Manufacturing process technology required	Your manufacturing technology
Socio-political factors in your environment	
Social attitudes and trends	Your company's responsiveness and flexibility

Table 6.1 – *cont.*

Laws and government agency regulations	Your company's ability to cope
Influence with pressure groups and government representatives	Your company's aggressiveness
Human factors, such as unionization and community acceptance	Your company's relationships

intends to go about achieving its objectives is strategy. Strategy is the overall route to the achievement of specific objectives and should describe the means by which objectives are to be reached, the time programme and the allocation of resources. It does not delineate the individual courses the resulting activity will follow.

There is a clear distinction between strategy, and detailed implementation or tactics. Marketing strategy reflects the company's best opinion as to how it can most profitably apply its skills and resources to the market place. It is inevitably broad in scope. The plan which stems from it will spell out action and timings and will contain the detailed contribution expected from each department.

There is a similarity between strategy in business and strategic military development. One looks at the enemy, the terrain, the resources under command, and then decides whether to attack the whole front, an area of enemy weakness, to feint in one direction while attacking in another, or to attempt an encirclement of the enemy's position. The policy and mix, the type of tactics to be used, and the criteria for judging success, all come under the heading of strategy. The action steps are tactics.

Table 6.2 Market attractiveness evaluation

Factor	Scoring criteria 10	5	0	Score	Weighting	Ranking
1 Market size (£m)	≥ £250	£51–250	≤ £50	5	15	0.75
2 Volume growth (units)	≥ 10%	5–9%	< 5%	10	25	2.5
3 Competitive intensity	Low	Medium	High	6	10	0.6
4 Industry profitability	> 15%	10–15%	< 10%	8	25	2.0
5 Vulnerability	Low	Medium	High	6	15	0.9
6 Cyclicality	Low	Medium	High	2.5	10	0.25
					Total =	7.0

This form illustrates a quantitative approach to evaluating market attractiveness. Each factor is the score multiplied by the percentage weighting and totalled for the overall score. In this example, an overall score of 7 out of 10 places this market in the highly attractive category.

Similarly, in marketing, the same commitment, mix and type of resources as well as tactical guidelines and criteria that must be met, all come under the heading of strategy.

For example, the decision to use distributors in all but the three largest market areas, in which company salesmen will be used, is a strategic decision. The selection of particular distributors is a tactical decision.

The following headings indicate the general content of strategy statements in the area of marketing which emerge from marketing literature:

1 Policies and procedures relating to the products to be offered, such as number, quality, design, branding, packaging and labelling, etc.
2 Pricing levels to be adopted, margins and discount policies.
3 Advertising and sales promotion. The creative approach, the type of media, type of displays, the amount to spend, etc.
4 What emphasis is to be placed on personal selling, the sales approach, sales training, etc.
5 The distributive channels to be used and the relative importance of each.
6 Warehousing, transportation, inventories, service levels, etc. in relation to distribution.

Thus, marketing strategies are the means by which marketing objectives will be achieved and are generally concerned with the four major elements of the marketing mix, as follows:

Product   The general policies for product deletions, modifications, additions, design, packing, etc.

Price   The general pricing policies to be followed for product groups in market segments.

Place   The general policies for channels and customer service levels.

Promotion The general policies for communicating with customers under the relevant headings, such as: advertising, sales force, sales promotion, public relations, exhibitions, direct mail, etc.

The following list of marketing strategies (in summary form), cover the majority of options open under the headings of the four Ps:

1 *Product*
   — expand the line
   — change performance, quality or features
   — consolidate the line

— standardize design
— positioning
— change the mix
— branding

2 *Price*
— change price, terms or conditions
— skimming policies
— penetration policies

3 *Promotion*
— change advertising or promotion
— change selling

4 *Place*
— change delivery or distribution
— change service
— change channels
— change the degree of forward integration

Chapters 7–10 are devoted to a much more detailed consideration of promotion, pricing and distribution. There is no chapter on product management because all the product options have been covered already, particularly in Chapter 5 in the discussion on the product audit.

There are further steps in the marketing planning process before detailed programmes are put together. These are estimating in broad terms the cost of the strategies, and delineating alternative plans. Both of these steps will be covered in more detail in Chapter 11.

Formulating marketing strategies is one of the most critical and difficult parts of the entire marketing process. It sets the limit of success. Communicated to all management levels, it indicates what strengths are to be developed, what weaknesses are to be remedied, and in what manner. Marketing strategies enable operating decisions to bring the company into the right relationship with the emerging pattern of market opportunities which previous analysis has shown to offer the highest prospect of success.

Before proceeding to describe the next stage of marketing planning, i.e. the construction of actual working plans, it should be stressed that the vital phase of setting objectives and strategies is a highly complex process which, if done badly, will probably result in considerable misdirection of resources.

This chapter has confirmed the need for setting clear, definitive objectives for all aspects of the marketing programme, and that marketing objectives themselves have to derive logically from corporate objectives. The advantages of this practice are that it allows all concerned with marketing activities to concentrate their particular contribution on achieving the overall marketing objectives, as well as facilitating meaningful and constructive evaluation of all marketing activity.

For the practical purpose of marketing planning, it will be apparent from the observations above concerning what was referred to as a hierarchy of objectives, that overall marketing objectives have to be broken down into sub-objectives which, taken all together, will achieve the overall objectives. By breaking down the overall objectives, the problem of strategy development becomes more manageable, hence easier.

A two-year study of 35 top industrial companies by McKinsey and Company revealed that leader companies agreed that product/market strategy is the key to the task of keeping shareholders' equity rising. Clearly, then, setting objectives and strategies in relation to products and markets is a most important step in the marketing planning process.

Once agreement has been reached on the broad marketing objectives and strategies, those responsible for programmes can now proceed to the detailed planning stage, developing the appropriate overall strategy statements into sub-objectives.

Plans constitute the vehicle for getting to the destination along the chosen route, or the detailed execution of the strategy. The term 'plan' is often used synonymously in marketing literature with the terms 'programme' and 'schedule'. A plan containing detailed lists of tasks to be completed, together with responsibilities, timing and cost, is sometimes referred to as an appropriation budget, which is merely a detailing of the actions to be carried out and of the expected sterling results in carrying them out. More about this in Chapters 7 to 10.

Application questions

1 Critically analyse your company's corporate objectives.
2 Critically analyse your company's corporate strategies.
3 Critically analyse your company's marketing objectives.
4 Critically analyse your company's marketing strategies.
5 Has there been any product/market extension during the past ten years which has not been compatible with your company's distinctive competence? If so, state why.
6 Draw up criteria for product/market extension which *are* compatible with your company's distinctive competences.

7 The Communication Plan: 1
The Advertising and Sales Promotion Plans

Now that we have explored the important area of marketing objectives and strategies, let us turn our attention to the question of how we communicate with customers, both current and potential.

It is a fact that company organizations communicate with their customers in a wide variety of ways, but it is still possible to distinguish the following two main categories:

1 *Impersonal communications*, e.g. advertising, point-of-sale displays, promotions, and public relations.
2 *Personal* (or direct person-to-person) *communications*, e.g. the face-to-face meeting between a salesman and his customer.

So companies have at their disposal an armoury of communication techniques which may be used either singly or in a combination (the 'communication mix') as the particular situation demands to achieve maximum effect within given budget constraints. Companies with acknowledged professionalism in the area of communicating with customers are continually experimenting with the mix of communicating techniques they employ in an attempt to become more cost-effective in this important, sometimes expensive, part of their business. A number of the possible means of communicating with customers will now be examined under the two broad headings given above. This chapter will look in more detail at advertising and sales promotion with the objective of deciding how to go about preparing detailed plans for these important elements of the marketing mix.

In Chapter 8 we will do the same for personal selling and the sales plan.

Deciding on the communications mix

Advertising is a popular method of impersonal communications using such media as the press, television, radio, billboard posters, and so on. However, there are a number of problems which need to be carefully considered before any decision can be made about whether to spend any money on advertising at all, let alone *how* to spend it. For example, many people believe that advertising is a waste of money and that media expenditure would be better spent on personal selling.

So the first question that has to be grappled with is the question of how to determine the communications mix. To help with this question, let us consider two separate surveys on how industry buys. These are shown in Tables 7.1 and 7.2.

Table 7.1   Buying influences by company size

Number of employees	Average number of buying influences	Average number of contacts made by salesmen
0–200	3.42	1.72
201–400	4.85	1.75
401–1000	5.81	1.90
1000+	6.50	1.65

Source: McGraw-Hill

Table 7.2   Sources of information

	% Small companies	% Large companies
Trade and technical press	28	60
Salesman—calls	47	19
Exhibitions	8	12
Direct mail	19	9

Source: Maclean Hunter

Even a cursory glance at these will reveal the following information:

1   More than one person has an influence on what is bought.
2   Salesmen do not manage to see all the important 'influencers'.
3   Companies get the information on which they make their decisions from a variety of sources, only one of which is the salesman.

It can be seen then that the buying process, but in particular the *industrial* buying process is complicated by the fact that it is not just one person who is involved. Industrial buying is a decision-making process which can involve a large number of people and take a considerable time. It is possible to split the decision-making process into several distinct steps, as follows:

1 The buyer organization recognizes it has a problem and works out a general solution. For example, the design team of a new plant or piece of machinery may decide that they need a specialist component which cannot be provided from within the company or from existing suppliers' stocks.
2 ïThe characteristics and quantity of what is needed are worked out. This is the outline design process specifying performance, and particular cħaracteristics such as weight, size, operating conditions, and so on.
3 A specification is then drawn up.
4 A search is made for possible sources of supply. This may merely involve a search of suppliers' catalogues to buy a component from stock, or a complete new product may have to be designed.
5 Potential suppliers will submit plans and products for evaluation.
6 After the necessary trials, suppliers are selected.
7 An order is placed and the product eventually delivered.
8 The goods supplied are checked against specification.

Not all these phases are followed in every buying decision. When something is being bought for a new project, all the phases would be followed.

Where it is a case of simply re-ordering something which has been bought before, the search and even tender processes may not be necessary. The newness of the decision to the buying organization also determines which types of people and how many are involved at each stage. Newness is a function of:

Complexity of the product.
Commercial uncertainty surrounding the outcome of the purchase.

The higher the 'newness' on both these dimensions, the more people are involved and the higher their status. If product complexity is high, but commercial uncertainty low, then the more important role is that of the design engineer and technologist. If newness is low on both dimensions, purchasing officers tend to dominate the process.

When faced with a new buy situation, the salesmen will be involved with a large number of people over a long period, helping, advising and informing, always trying to influence the decision process and to build up a growing commitment towards his product. A typical example of this process at work can be seen in the following example of the purchase of a telecommunications system:

1 The Managing Director proposes to replace the company's telecommunications system.
2 Corporate purchasing and corporate telecommunications departments
   analyse the company's needs and recommend likely matches with potential selling organizations.
3 Corporate telecommunications department and data processing managers have an important say about which system and firm the company
   will deal with. Other company directors also have a key influence on this
   decision.
4 All employees who use the telecommunications equipment are 'con-
   sulted'.
5 The Director of Administration selects, with influence from others, the
   supplying company and the system.

The reason for going into such detail about the industrial buying process is
simply to illustrate that it is not possible to determine the precise role of
advertising versus, say, personal selling, until a company fully understands
how its potential customers buy and who are the important people that have
to be contacted at the different stages in the buying process. For clearly,
financial and administrative people will be involved at a different stage from,
say, the engineers, and they will also require different kinds of information.
For example, price, performance characteristics, delivery, before and after
sales service, reputation/reliability, guarantees, payment terms, and so on,
are not relevant to all people at all stages in the buying process.

The first point, then, is that a firm must understand the buying process of
the markets to which it addresses itself. There are many models for helping
with this process, but essentially we should use a simple model which
answers these questions:

1 Who are the people with a significant influence on the purchase decision?
2 What specific *benefits* does each important influencer want?

Having done this analysis for our major customers/potential customers, it
should be comparatively easy to:

1 Group them in some way (segmentation).
2 Determine the most cost-effective way of communicating these benefits
   to each group.

Only then can some qualitative judgements be made about the relative
cost-effectiveness of, say, advertising versus personal selling, neither of
which, incidentally, will be mutually exclusive in anything but unusual
circumstances. Table 7.3 lists some communication objectives.

Table 7.3 Some communication objectives

Education and information	To . . .	
	Create awareness	
	Inform	
	Get enquiries	These objectives
Branding and	Get company name in file	contribute
image	Create company image	towards a total
building	Reach personnel	marketing
	inaccessible to salesmen	programme, the
Affecting	Ease the selling task	objective of
attitudes	Get editorial	which is to
	Overcome prejudice	achieve
	Influence end-users	profitable
Loyalty and	Reduce selling costs	sales
reminding	Achieve sales	

We can now turn our attention to advertising specifically.

Preparing the advertising plan

For many years people believed that advertising worked in a delightfully simple way, with the advertiser sending a message and the target receiving it and understanding it. Research, however, has shown that in a grossly over-communicated society, the process is more complex. Figure 7.1 gives some indication of the process involved.

Advertising, then, is not the straightforward activity that many people believe it to be. It is highly unlikely, for example, that any firm will be able simply to put out an advertisement and expect their sales to increase.

This brings us to perhaps the greatest misconception of all about advertising—that objectives for advertising for the purpose of measuring effectiveness should be set in terms of sales increases. Naturally, we hope that advertising will have an important influence on sales levels, but in most circumstances advertising is only one of a whole host of important determinants of sales levels (such as product quality, prices, customer service levels, the competence of the sales force, and so on). Generally, then, it is absurd to set sales increases as an objective for advertising.

So what objectives should be set for advertising? Well, we can start by agreeing that we need to *set* objectives for advertising, for the following reasons:

1   We need to set the budget for advertising. Therefore we need some objectives.

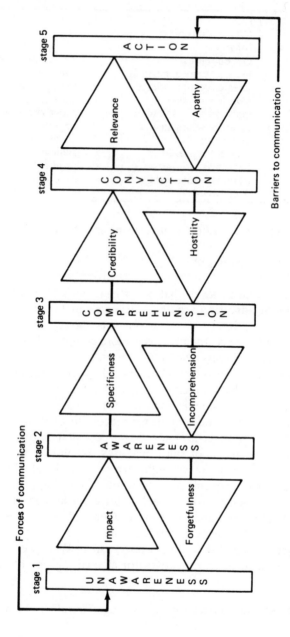

Figure 7.1   Brand loyalty ladder: the five stages of communication.

2   We need to determine who our target audience is. Therefore we need some objectives.
3   We need to determine the content of advertisements. Therefore we need some objectives.
4   We need to decide on what media to use. Therefore we need some objectives.
5   We need to decide on the frequency of advertising. Therefore we need some objectives.
6   We need to decide how to measure the effectiveness of our advertising. Therefore we need some objectives.

These decisions can be summarized as follows:

1   *Why* (objectives)
2   *Who* (target)
3   *What* (copy platform)
4   *Where* (media)
5   *How* (creative platform)
6   *When* (timing)
7   *How much* (budget)
8   *Schedule*
9   *Response*
10 *Evaluation*

The whole edifice, however, depends on the first of these.

Advertising objectives

Research has shown that many companies set objectives for advertising which advertising cannot achieve on its own. Apart from increasing sales, the 'annihilation of the enemy' and other such ridiculously unachievable objectives are set. For example, it is unreasonable to set as an objective 'to convince our target market that our product is best' if it is perfectly clear to the whole world that someone else's product is better. You cannot blame your advertising agency if this objective is not achieved!

Another example of inadequate thought being given to advertising expenditure was the bus company who spent vast sums advertising the reliability of their bus service, while research showed the real reason sales were deteriorating was that many people thought buses were 'working class'. Again, this is a classic example of scoring a bulls-eye at the wrong target.

The first step, then, is to decide on reasonable objectives for advertising. The question which must be asked is: 'Is it possible to achieve the objective through advertising alone?' If the answer is *yes*, it is an objective for advertising. If the answer is *no*, it is not an objective for advertising. Advertising through media can do the following:

Convey information
Alter perceptions/attitudes
Create desires
Establish connections (e.g. powdered cream/coffee)
Direct actions
Provide reassurance
Remind
Give reasons for buying
Demonstrate
Generate enquiries

Setting reasonable, achievable objectives then is the first and most important step in the advertising plan. All the other steps in the process of putting together the advertising plan flow naturally from this and are summarized briefly below.

Who   . . . are the target audience(s)?
           What do they already know, feel, believe about us and our product/service?
           What do they know, feel, believe about the competition?
           What sort of people are they? How do we describe/identify them?

What   . . . response do we wish to evoke from the target audience(s)?
           . . . are these specific communications *objectives*?
           . . . do we want to 'say', make them 'feel', 'believe', 'understand', 'know' about buying/using our product/service?
           . . . are we offering?
           . . . do we *not* want to convey?
           . . . are the priorities of importance of our objectives?
           . . . are the objectives *written* down and *agreed* by the Company and Advertising Agency?

How   . . . are our objectives to be embodied in an appealing form?
           What is our creative strategy/platform?
           What evidence do we have that this is acceptable and appropriate to our audience(s)?

Where   . . . is the most cost-effective place(s) to expose our communications (in cost terms *vis-à-vis* our audience)?
. . . is the most beneficial place(s) for our communications (in expected response terms *vis-à-vis* the 'quality' of the channels available)?

When   . . . are our communications to be displayed/conveyed to our audience?
What is the reasoning for our scheduling of advertisements/communications over time?
What constraints limit our freedom of choice?
Do we have to fit in with other promotional activity on
— our products/services supplied by our company?
— other products/services supplied by our company?
— competitors' products?
— seasonal trends?
— special events in the market?

Result   What results do we expect?
How would we measure results?
Do we intend to measure results and, if so, do we need to do anything *beforehand*?
If we cannot say how we would measure precise results, then maybe our *objectives* are not sufficiently specific or are not communications objectives?
How are we going to judge the relative success of our communications activities (good-bad-indifferent)?
Should we have action standards?

Budget   How much money do the intended activities need?
How much money is going to be made available?
How are we going to *control* expenditure?

Schedule Who is to do what and when?
What is being spent on what, where and when?

The usual assumption is that advertising is deployed in an aggressive role and that all that changes over time is the creative content. But the role of advertising usually changes during the life cycle of a product.

For example, the process of persuasion itself cannot usually start until there is some level of awareness about a product or service in the market place. Creating awareness is, therefore, usually one of the most important objectives early on in a life cycle. If awareness has been created, interest in learning more will usually follow.

Attitude development now begins in earnest. This might also involve reinforcing an existing attitude or even changing previously held attitudes in order to clear the way for a new purchase. This role obviously tends to become more important later in the product life cycle, when competitive products are each trying to establish their own 'niche' in the market.

Diffusion of innovation

Also relevant to this is what is known as the 'diffusion of innovation'. Diffusion is:

1 The adoption
2 of new products or services
3 over time
4 by consumers
5 within social systems
6 as encouraged by marketing activities

Diffusion refers to the cumulative percentage of potential adopters of a new product or service over time. Everett Rogers examined some of the social forces that explain the product life cycle. The body of knowledge often referred to as 'reference theory' (which incorporates work on group norms, group pressures and the like), helps explain the snowball effect of diffusion. Rogers found that the actual rate of diffusion is a function of a product's:

I   *Relative advantage* (over existing products)
II   *Compatability* (with life styles, values, etc.)
III *Communicability* (is it easy to communicate?)
IV   *Complexity* (is it complicated?)
V   *Divisibility* (can it be tried out on a small scale before commitment?)

Diffusion is also a function of the newness of the product itself, which can be classified broadly under three headings:

Continuous innovation (e.g. the new miracle ingredient)
Dynamically continuous innovation (e.g. disposable lighter)
Discontinuous (e.g. microwave oven)

However, Rogers found that for all new products, not everyone adopts new products at the same time, and that a universal pattern emerged, shown in Figure 7.2.

In general, the innovators think for themselves and try new things (where relevant); the early adopters, who have status in society, are opinion leaders

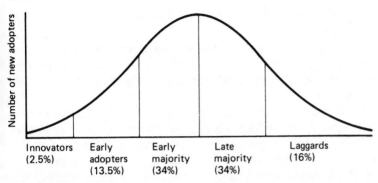

Figure 7.2

and they adopt successful products, making them acceptable and respectable; the early majority, who are more conservative and who have slightly above average status, are more deliberate and only adopt products that have social approbation; the late majority, who are below average status and more sceptical, adopt products much later; the laggards, with low status, income, etc., view life through the rear mirror and are the last to adopt products.

This particular piece of research can be very useful, particularly for advertising and personal selling. For example, if we can develop a typology for innovative customers, we can target our early advertising and sales effort specifically at them. Once the first 3 per cent of innovators have adopted our product, there is a good chance that the early adopters will try it, and once the 10–12 per cent point is reached, the champagne can be opened, because there is a good chance that the rest will adopt our product.

We know, for example, that the *general* characteristics of opinion leaders are that they are: venturesome; socially integrated; cosmopolitan; socially mobile; and privileged. So we need to ask ourselves what are the *specific* characteristics of these customers in our particular industry. We can then tailor our advertising message specifically for them.

Finally, we should remind ourselves that advertising is not directed only at consumers. It can be directed at channels, shareholders, media, employees, suppliers and government, all of whom have an important influence on a firm's commercial success.

Sales promotion

The term *advertising* (often referred to as 'above-the-line expenditure') can be defined as all non-personal communication in measured media. This includes television, cinema, radio, print, and outdoor media.

Sales promotion, for which the term 'below-the-line expenditure' is often used as a synonym, is not so easily defined. For example, the Americans use the term to describe all forms of communication, including advertising and personal selling. In Britain some use the term to describe any non-face-to-face activity concerned with the promotion of sales; some use it to describe any non-media expenditure; while others use it specifically to mean in-store merchandising.

The fact is that none of these definitions is an accurate reflection of how sales promotion works in practice, which is why there is so much confusion about many aspects of this important area of marketing activity.

In practice, sales promotion is a specific activity, which can be defined as the making of a featured offer to defined customers within a specific time limit. In other words, to qualify as a sales promotion, someone must be offered something which is featured, rather than just being an aspect of trade. Furthermore, the offer must include benefits not inherent in the product or service, as opposed to the intangible benefits offered in advertising, such as adding value through appeals to imagery.

Seen this way, every other element of the marketing mix, including advertising, personal selling, point-of-sale material, pricing, after-sales service, and so on, can be used as part of a structured activity in order to achieve specified objectives.

How can we use sales promotion?

Sales promotion is essentially a problem-solving activity designed to get customers to behave more in line with the economic interests of the company. Typical tasks for sales promotion are: slow stock movement; counteracting competitive activity; encouraging repeat purchase; securing marginal buyers; getting bills paid on time; inducing trial purchase; and so on.

From this it will be seen that sales promotion is not necessarily concerned with volume increases. For example, it is often used to assist production and distribution scheduling by persuading customers to bring forward their peak buying from one period to another. To summarize, sales promotion seeks to influence:

Salesmen	to sell	
Customers	to buy	
Customers	to sell	more, earlier, faster, etc.
Users	to buy	
Users	to use	

Although in recent years sales promotion activity has increased to such an extent that it now accounts for as much expenditure as above-the-line advertising, it is important to realize that on its own sales promotion will not replace selling, change long-term trends, or build you long-term customer loyalty. Nevertheless while sales promotion is essentially a tactical device, it also has an important strategic role to play as we shall see later.

What different kinds of sales promotion are there?

The many and varied types of sales promotions are listed in Table 7.4. Each of these different types is appropriate for different circumstances and each has advantages and disadvantages. For example, with a promotion that consists of a free case bonus, it is possible to measure precisely both the cost of the extra cases and the additional volume resulting from the offer; it is fast and flexible; it is effective where the customer is profit conscious; it can be

Table 7.4   Types of sales promotions

Target Market	Money		Goods		Services	
	Direct	Indirect	Direct	Indirect	Direct	Indirect
Consumer	Price reduction	Coupons Vouchers Money equivalent Competitions	Free goods offers (e.g. 13 for 12) Free gifts Trade-in offers	Stamps Coupons Vouchers Money equivalent Competitions	Guarantees Group participation Special exhibitions and displays	Cooperative advertising Stamps, coupons Vouchers for services Events admission Competitions
Trade	Dealer loaders Loyalty schemes Incentives Full-range buying	Extended credit Delayed invoicing Sale or return Coupons Vouchers Money equivalent	Free gifts Trial offers Trade-in offers	Coupons Vouchers Money equivalent Competitions	Guarantees Group participation events Free services Risk reduction schemes Training Special exhibitions, displays Demonstrations Reciprocal trading schemes	Stamps, coupons Vouchers for services Competitions
Sales force	Bonus Commission	Coupons Vouchers Points systems Money equivalent Competitions	Free gifts	Coupons Vouchers Points systems Money equivalent	Free services Group participation events	Coupons Vouchers Points systems for services Event admission Competitions

made to last as long as required; and it is simple to set up, administer and sell. On the other hand, it has no cumulative value to the customer, is unimaginative, and can often be seen as a prelude to a permanent price reduction.

Points schemes are flexible, have wide appeal, do not involve the company in holding stocks of gifts, customers cannot easily value gifts, and they are easy to administer. On the other hand, they offer no advantages in bulk buying, are difficult to budget; and they lack the immediacy of dealer loaders.

Great care is necessary, therefore, in selecting a scheme appropriate to the objective sought.

Strategic role of sales promotion

Because sales promotion is essentially used as a tactical device, it often amounts to little more than a series of spasmodic gimmicks lacking in any coherence. Yet the same management that organizes sales promotion usually believes that advertising should conform to some overall strategy. Perhaps this is because advertising has always been based on a philosophy of building long-term brand franchise in a consistent manner, whereas the basic rationale of sales promotion is to help the company retain a tactical initiative.

Even so, there is no reason why there should not be a strategy for sales promotion, so that each promotion increases the effectiveness of the next, so that a bond between seller and buyer is built up, so that the tactical objectives are linked in with some overall plan, and so that there is generally a better application of resources.

That this is possible can be seen from the sales promotional campaigns involving the Home Pride Flour Graders, who first appeared in the early sixties, from the 20 million enamel Golly brooches given out by Robertsons since the nineteen thirties, from Mighty Ajax, Miss Pears, the Ovaltineys, and many other campaigns which have used schemes and devices which have been consistently incorporated into a product's promotional strategy.

More recent schemes, such as the Esso tiger, and the Smurfs of BP, are proof that it is possible to establish a style of promotion which, if consistently applied, will help to establish the objectives of a product over a long period of time, which are flexible, and which have staying power.

Can sales promotion be applied to industrial products?

Industrial goods are always sold to other organizations and this has the effect of changing the emphasis placed on certain elements of the marketing mix rather than having any fundamental effect on the relevancy of the marketing concept.

It will not be surprising then to learn that, suitably adapted, most consumer goods sales promotional techniques can be applied to industrial goods. Yet in spite of this, sales promotion is comparatively rare in industrial markets, perhaps partly from a belief born in the engineering discipline that if a firm has to promote its products, there must be something wrong with them.

In recent years, however, industrial goods companies have begun to take note of the enormous success of campaigns such as Yorkshire Imperial Metal's Golden Spanner, the schemes of the Herbert Morris Group, and others, and are becoming more aware of sales promotion as a flexible and competitive tool of marketing. 3M recently offered a cash redemption coupon to prospective buyers of photocopiers via an advertisement in a Sunday newspaper. One industrial goods company with divisions spanning a range of products from fast-moving industrial goods to high-priced capital goods has developed a range of special promotional schemes which include the following: trade-in allowances; competitions; reciprocal trading schemes; credit arrangements; training schemes; desk-top give-aways; custom-built guarantees—all made as featured offers.

Preparing the sales promotion plan

There is widespread acknowledgement that sales promotion is one of the most mismanaged of all marketing functions. This is mainly because of the confusion about what sales promotion is, which often results in expenditures not being properly recorded. Some companies include it with advertising, others as part of sales force expenditure, others as a general marketing expense, others as a manufacturing expense (as in the case of extra product, or special labels, or packaging), while the loss of revenue from special price reductions is often not recorded at all.

Such failures can be extremely damaging because sales promotion is such an important part of marketing strategy. Also, with increasing competition from Common Market countries, troubled economic conditions, and growing pressures from the trade, sales promotion is becoming more widespread and more acceptable. This means that companies can no longer afford not to set objectives, or to evaluate results after the event, or to fail to have some company guidelines. For example, a £1 case allowance on a product with a contribution rate of £3 per case has to increase sales by 50 per cent just to maintain the same level of contribution. Failure at least to realize this, or to set alternative objectives for the promotion, can easily result in loss of control and a consequent reduction in profits.

In order to manage a company's sales promotion expenditure more effectively, there is one essential step that must be taken. First, an objective for sales promotion must be established in the same way that an objectives is developed for advertising, pricing, or distribution. The objectives for each promotion should be clearly stated, such as trial, repeat purchase, distribution, display, a shift in buying peaks, combating competition, and so on. Thereafter, the following process should apply:

Select the appropriate technique
Pretest
Mount the promotion
Evaluate in depth

Spending must be analysed and categorized by type of activity (e.g. special packaging, special point-of-sale material, loss of revenue through price reductions, and so on).

One company manufacturing self-assembly kitchens embarked on a heavy programme of sales promotion after a dramatic reduction in consumer demand. While they managed to maintain turnover, they were worried that their sales promotional activities had been carried out in such a haphazard and piecemeal fashion that they were unable to evaluate the cost-effectiveness of what they had done. They were also very concerned about its effect on company image and their long-term consumer franchise. So the company made a concentrated study of this area of expenditure, which now represented over half their communication budget. Next time round they had: clear objectives; a clear promotional plan properly integrated into the marketing plan; an established means of assessment.

As for the sales promotional plan itself, the objectives, strategy and brief details of timing and costs should be included. It is important that too much detail should *not* appear in the sales promotional plan. Detailed promotional instructions will follow as the marketing plan unfurls. For example, the following checklist outlines the kind of detail that should eventually be circulated. However, only an outline of this should appear in the marketing plan itself.

Checklist for promotional instruction

Heading	Content
1 *Introduction*	Briefly summarize content—what? where? when?
2 *Objectives*	Marketing and promotional for new product launch
3 *Background*	Market data. Justification for technique. Other relevant matters.

4	*Promotional offer*	Detail the offer: special pricing structure; describe premium; etc. Be brief, precise and unambiguous.
5	*Eligibility*	Who? Where?
6	*Timing*	When is the offer available? Call, delivery or invoice dates?
7	*Date plan*	Assign dates and responsibilities for all aspects of plan prior to start date.
8	*Support*	Special advertising, point of sale, presenters, leaflets etc., public relations, samples, etc.
9	*Administration*	Invoicing activity. Free goods invoice lines. Depot stocks. Premium (re)ordering procedure. Cash drawing procedures.
10	*Sales plan*	Targets. Incentives. Effect on routing. Briefing meetings. Telephone sales.
11	*Sales presentation*	Points to be covered in call.
12	*Sales reporting*	Procedure for collection of required data not otherwise available.
13	*Assessment*	How will the promotion be evaluated?

Appendices
Usually designed to be carried by salesmen as an aid to selling the promotion:

Summary of presentation points
Price structures/profit margins
Summary of offer
Schedules of qualifying orders
Blank order forms for suggested orders
Copies of leaflets

Also required by the salesforce may be:

Samples of (new) product
Demonstration specimen of premium item
Special report forms
Returns of cash/premiums etc. issued

NB It is assumed that the broad principles of the promotion have already been agreed by the Sales Manager.

Application questions

1 How does your company determine its communications mix (i.e. the relative emphasis given to advertising, sales promotion and personal selling)?
2 Describe the buying process in one of your major customer groups. Who are the key influencers? Critically appraise your strategy for communicating with them.
3 Critically appraise your advertising objectives.
4 Using the checklist given in the text, critically appraise your advertising plan.
5 Where you launch a new product/service, do you target your communications specifically at the innovators? Do you know who they are? Can you describe them in terms that are relevant to advertising?
6 Critically evaluate your sales promotional plan.
7 How do you evaluate your sales promotional activities?

8 The Communication Plan: 2
The Sales Plan

Personal selling has an important strategic role to play in communicating between a company and its customers. To have a chance of success, management must be able to answer the following kinds of question:

How important is personal selling?
What is the role of personal selling in the marketing mix?
How many salesmen do we need?
What do we want them to do?
How should they be managed?

These and other questions will be considered in this chapter as important determinants of the sales plan.

How important is personal selling?

Most organizations had an organized sales force long before they introduced a formal marketing activity of the kind described throughout this text. In spite of this fact, sales force management has traditionally been a neglected area of marketing management.

There are several possible reasons. One is that not all marketing and product managers have had experience in a personal selling or sales management role; consequently, these managers often underestimate the importance of efficient personal selling.

Another reason for neglect of sales force management is that sales personnel themselves sometimes encourage an unhelpful distinction between sales and marketing by depicting themselves as 'the sharp end'. After all, isn't there something slightly daring about dealing with real live customers as opposed to sitting in an office surrounded by marketing surveys, charts and plans? That such reasoning is misleading will be obvious because unless a good deal of careful marketing planning has taken place before the salesman makes his effort to persuade the customer to place an order, the probability of a successful sale is much reduced.

The suggested distinction between marketing 'theory' and sales 'practice' is further invalidated when we consider that profitable sales depend not just on individual customers and individual products but on groups of customers (that is, market segments) and on the supportive relationship of products to each other (that is, a carefully planned product portfolio). Another factor to be taken into account in this context is the constant need for the organization to think in terms of where future sales will be coming from rather than to concentrate solely on present products, customers and problems.

The author of this text has investigated many European sales forces over the last decade and has found an alarming lack of planning and professionalism. Salesmen frequently have little idea of which products and which groups of customers to concentrate on, have too little knowledge about competitive activity, do not plan presentations well, rarely talk to customers in terms of *benefits*, make too little effort to close the sale, and make many calls without any clear objectives. Even worse, marketing management is rarely aware that this important and expensive element of the marketing mix is not being managed effectively. The fact that many organizations have separate departments and directors for the marketing and sales activities increases the likelihood of such failures of communication.

Although its importance varies according to circumstances, in many businesses the sales force is the most important element in the marketing mix. In industrial goods companies, for example, it is not unusual to find very small amounts being spent on other forms of communication and very large sums being spent on the sales force in the form of salaries, cars and associated costs.

Personal selling is also used widely in many service industries where customers are looking for very specific benefits. Insurance companies, for example, do use media advertising but rely for most of their sales on personal selling. Customers for insurance policies almost invariably need to discuss which policy would best fit their particular needs and circumstances; it is the task of the salesman to explain the choices available and to suggest the most appropriate policy.

Recent surveys show that more money is spent by companies on their sales forces than on advertising and sales promotion combined. Personal selling, then, is a vital and expensive element in the marketing mix.

The solution to the problem of poor sales force management can only be found in the recognition that personal selling is indeed a crucial part of the marketing process but that it must be planned and considered as carefully as any other element. Indeed, it is an excellent idea for any manager responsible for marketing to go out into a territory for a few days each year and himself attempt to persuade customers to place orders. It is a good way of finding out what customers really think of the organization's marketing policies!

Role of personal selling

Personal selling can be seen most usefully as part of the *communications mix*. (Other common elements of the communications mix, it will be remembered, are advertising, sales promotion, public relations, direct mail, exhibitions, and so on.) The surveys set out in Chapter 7 show that organizations cannot leave the communications task only to the sales force. The same question remains, however, as with advertising. This is how the organization is to define the role of personal selling in its communications mix. Again, the answer lies in a clear understanding of the buying process which operates in the company's markets.

The efficiency of any element of communication depends on achieving a match between information required and information given. To achieve this match, the marketer must be aware of the different requirements of different people at different stages of the buying process. This approach highlights the importance of ensuring that the company's communications reach *all* key points in the buying chain. No company can afford to assume that the actual sale is the only important event.

In order to determine the precise role of personal selling in its communications mix, the company must identify the major influencers in each purchase decision and find out what information they are likely to need at different stages of the buying process. Most institutional buying decisions consist of many separate phases, from the recognition of a problem through to performance evaluation and feedback on the product or service purchased. Furthermore, the importance of each of these phases varies according to whether the buying situation is a first-time purchase or a routine repurchase. Clearly, the information needs will differ in each case. (This was discussed in some detail in Chapter 7.)

Personal selling has a number of advantages over other elements of the communications mix:

1   It is a two-way form of communication, giving the prospective purchaser the opportunity to ask questions of the salesmen about the product or service.
2   The sales message itself can be made more flexible and therefore can be more closely tailored to the needs of individual customers.

3 The salesman can use in-depth product knowledge to relate his message to the perceived needs of the buyer and to deal with objections as they arise.

4 Most importantly, the salesman can ask for an order and, perhaps, negotiate on price, delivery or special requirements.

Once an order has been obtained from a customer and there is a high probability of a re-buy occurring, the salesman's task changes from persuasion to reinforcement. All communications at this stage should contribute to underlining the wisdom of the purchase. The salesman may also take the opportunity to encourage consideration of other products or services in the company's range.

Clearly, in different markets different weighting is given to the various forms of communication available. In the grocery business, for example, advertising and sales promotion are extremely important elements in the communications process. However, the food manufacturer must maintain an active sales force which keeps in close contact with the retail buyers. This retail contact ensures vigorous promotional activity in the chain. In the wholesale hardware business frequent and regular face-to-face contact with retail outlets through a sales force is the key determinant of success. In industries where there are few customers (such as capital goods and specialized process materials) an in-depth understanding of the customers' production processes has to be built up; here, again, personal contact is of paramount importance. In contrast, many fast-moving industrial goods are sold into fragmented markets for diverse uses; in this area forms of communication other than personal selling take on added importance.

Many companies in the electronics business use personal selling to good advantage. Word processors, for example, vary enormously in the range of capabilities they offer. Technical details can be supplied in brochures and other promotional material, but the administrative staff likely to be taking the purchase decision often find it difficult to evaluate the alternatives. A good salesman can ascertain quickly the requirements of a particular client and identify to what extent these will be fulfilled by his equipment. For his part, the customer can identify quickly whether the company understands his requirements, whether it appears credible, and whether or not it is able to provide the back-up service necessary to install the equipment and establish its use in the organization. Such considerations are likely to be far more influential than the comparison of technical data sheets in a decision to purchase.

How many salesmen do we need?

The organization should begin its consideration of how many salesmen it needs by finding out exactly how work is allocated at present. Start by listing all the things the current sales force actually does. These might include opening new accounts; servicing existing accounts; demonstrating new products; taking repeat orders; and collecting debts. This listing should be followed by investigation of alternative ways of carrying out these responsibilities. For example, telephone selling has been shown to be a perfectly acceptable alternative to personal visits, particularly in respect of repeat business. The sales force can thus be freed for missionary work, which is not so susceptible to the telephone approach. Can debts be collected by mail or by telephone? Can products be demonstrated at exhibitions or showrooms? It is only by asking these kinds of question that we can be certain we have not fallen into the common trap of committing the company to a decision and then seeking data and reasons to justify the decision. At this stage, the manager should concentrate on collecting relevant, quantified data and then use judgement and experience to help him come to a decision.

Basically, all sales force activities can be categorized under three headings. A salesman:

— makes calls
— travels
— performs administrative functions

These tasks constitute what can be called his *workload*. If we first decide what constitutes a reasonable workload for a salesman, in hours per month, then we can begin to measure how long his current activities take, hence the exact extent of his current workload.

This measurement can be performed either by some independent third party or, preferably, by the salesmen themselves. All they have to do for one simple method of measurement is to record distance travelled, time in and out of calls, and the outlet type. This data can then be analysed easily to indicate the average duration of a call by outlet type, the average distance travelled in a month, and the average speed according to the nature of the territory (that is, city, suburbs or country). With the aid of a map, existing customers can be allocated on a trial-and-error basis, together with the concomitant time values for clerical activities and travel. In this way, equitable workloads can be calculated for the sales force, building in, if necessary, spare capacity for sometimes investigating potential new sales outlets.

This kind of analysis sometimes produces surprising results, as when the company's 'star' salesman is found to have a smaller workload than the one with the worst results, who may be having to work much longer hours to achieve his sales because of the nature of his territory.

There are, of course, other ways of measuring workloads. One major consumer goods company used its Work Study Department to measure sales force effectiveness. The results of this study are summarized in Table 8.1.

Table 8.1 Breakdown of a salesman's total daily activity

		Per cent of day	Minutes per day
Outside call time	Drive to and from route	15.9	81
	Drive on route	16.1	83
	Walk	4.6	24
	Rest and breaks	6.3	32
	Pre-call administration	1.4	7
	Post-call administration	5.3	27
		49.6	254
Inside call time	Business talks	11.5	60
	Sell	5.9	30
	Chat	3.4	17
	Receipts	1.2	6
	Miscellaneous	1.1	6
	Drink	1.7	8
	Waiting	7.1	36
		31.9	163
Evening work	Depot work	9.8	50
	Entering pinks	3.9	20
	Pre-plan route	4.8	25
		18.5	95
		100.0	8 hr 32 min

The table showed the company how a salesman's time was spent and approximately how much of his time was actually available for selling. One immediate action taken by the company was to initiate a training programme which enabled more time to be spent on selling as a result of better planning. Another was to improve the quality of the sales performance while face-to-face with the customers.

Armed with this kind of quantitative data, it becomes easier to determine how many salesmen are needed and how territories can be equitably allocated.

What do we want our salesmen to do?

Whatever the method used to organize the salesman's day, there is always comparatively little time available for selling. In these circumstances, it is vital that a company should know as precisely as possible what it wants its sales force to do. Sales force objectives can be either *quantitative* or *qualitative*.

Quantitative objectives

Principal quantitative objectives are concerned with the following measures:

How much to sell (the value of unit sales volume)
What to sell (the mix of product lines to sell)
Where to sell (the markets and individual customers that will take the company towards its marketing objectives)
Desired profit contribution (where relevant and where the company is organized to compute this)
Selling costs (in compensation, expenses, supervision, and so on)

The first three types of objectives are derived directly from the marketing objectives, which are discussed in detail in Chapter 6, and constitute the principal components of the sales plan.

There are, of course, many other kinds of quantitative objectives which can be set for the sales force, including the following:

Number of point-of-sale displays organized
Number of letters written to prospects
Number of telephone calls to prospects
Number of reports turned or not turned in
Number of trade meetings held
Use of sales aids in presentations
Number of service calls made
Number of customer complaints
Safety record
Collections made
Training meetings conducted
Competitive activity reports
General market condition reports

Salesmen may also be required to fulfil a co-ordinating role between a team of specialists and the client organization. A company selling mining machinery, for example, employs a number of 'good general salesmen' who establish contacts and identify which contacts are likely to lead to sales.

Before entering into negotiations with any client organization, the company selling the machinery may feel that it needs to call in a team of highly specialized engineers and financial experts for consultation and advice. It is the task of the salesman in this company to identify when specialist help is needed and to co-ordinate the people who become involved in the negotiation. However, most objectives are subservient to the major objectives outlined above which are associated directly with what is sold and to whom.

Qualitative objectives

Qualitative objectives can be a potential source of problems if sales managers try to assess the performance of the sales force along dimensions which include abstract terms such as 'loyalty', 'enthusiasm', 'co-operation', and so on, since such terms are difficult to measure objectively. In seeking qualitative measurements of performance, managers often resort to highly subjective interpretations which cause resentment and frustration among those being assessed.

However, managers can set and measure qualitative objectives which actually relate to the performance of the sales force on the job. It is possible, for example, to assess the skill with which a person applies his product knowledge on the job, or the skill with which he plans his work, or the skill with which he overcomes objections during a sales interview. While still qualitative in nature, these measures relate to standards of performance understood and accepted by the sales force.

Given such standards, it is not too difficult for a competent field sales manager to identify deficiencies, to get agreement on them, to coach in skills and techniques, to build attitudes of professionalism, to show how to self-train, to determine which training requirements cannot be tackled in the field, and to evaluate improvements in performance and the effect of any past training.

One consumer goods company with thirty field sales managers discovered that most of them were spending much of the day in their offices engaged in administrative work, most of it self-made. The company proceeded to take the offices away and insisted that the sales managers spend most of their time in the field training their salesmen. To assist them in this task, they trained them how to appraise and improve salesmen's performance in the field. There was a dramatic increase in sales and consequently in the sales managers' own earnings. This rapidly overcame their resentment at losing their offices.

How should we manage our sales force?

Sales force motivation has received a great deal of attention in recent times, largely as a result of the work done by psychologists in other fields of management. There is now widespread appreciation of the fact that it is not sufficient merely to give someone a title and an office and expect to get good results. Effective leadership, it is acknowledged, is as much 'follower-determined' as it is determined by management. While for the purposes of this discussion it is not necessary to enter into a detailed discussion of sales force motivation, it is worth mentioning briefly some important factors that contribute to effective sales force management.

If a sales manager's job is to improve the performance of his sales force, and if performance is a function of incentives minus disincentives, then the more he can increase incentives and reduce disincentives, the better will be performance.

Research has shown that an important element of sales force motivation is a sense of doing a worthwhile job. In other words, desire for praise and recognition, the avoidance of boredom and monotony, the enhancement of self-image, freedom from fear and worry, and the desire to belong to something believed to be worthwhile, all contribute to enhanced performance. One well-known piece of research carried out in the USA examined the reasons for the results of the twenty highest producing sales units in one company compared with the twenty lowest producing sales units. The research showed all the above factors to be major determinants of success.

However, remuneration will always be a most important determinant of motivation. This does not necessarily mean paying the most money, although clearly unless there are significant financial motivations within a company, it is unlikely that people will stay. In drawing up a remuneration plan, which would normally include a basic salary plus some element for special effort, such as bonus or commission, the following objectives should be considered:

To attract and keep effective salesmen.
To remain competitive.
To reward salesmen in accordance with their individual performance.
To provide a guaranteed income plus an orderly individual growth rate.
To generate individual sales initiative.
To encourage teamwork.
To encourage the performance of essential non-selling tasks.
To ensure that management can fairly administer and adjust compensation levels as a means of achieving sales objectives.

A central concept of sales force motivation is that the individual salesman will exert more effort if he is led to concentrate on:

1 His expectations of accomplishing his sales objectives.
2 The personal benefits derived from accomplishing those objectives.

This theory of sales force motivation is known as the path-goal approach because it is based on the particular path the salesman follows to a particular sales objective and the particular goals associated with successfully travelling down that path. The salesman estimates the probability of success of travelling down various paths or sales approaches and estimates the probability that his superiors will recognize his goal accomplishments and will reward him accordingly. Stated less formally, the motivational functions of the sales manager consist of increasing personal pay-offs to salesmen for work-goal attainment, making the path to these pay-offs easier to travel by clarifying it, reducing road blocks and pitfalls, and increasing the opportunities for personal satisfaction *en route*.

Few people would deny that sales force motivation is a difficult and highly emotive subject, and at the end of the day commonsense must prevail. The writer once attended a sales conference which opened with large-busted girls dancing to the company song. They were followed immediately by a tawdry-looking marketing manager who spent an hour pointing to bar charts on an overhead projector. Not surprisingly, few salesmen remembered much about the central issues of the conference!

Another common feature of sales conferences is the use of bellicose language, such as 'our plan is to wipe out the enemy . . .' and so on. The use of such imagery is often in sharp contrast to the day-to-day circumstances of the average salesman, who gets up on a rainy Monday morning, gets into his small company car, and is rejected on his first call of the week!

A bit of excitement at sales conferences is necessary, of course, but most sales directors and managers would be better occupied providing the sales force with information and tools designed to make the selling task easier. Naked ladies jumping out of giant cans may well have a place somewhere, but not, maybe, at sales conferences!

Preparing the sales plan

No two sales plans will contain precisely the same headings. However, some general guidelines can be given. Table 8.2 is an example of setting objectives for an individual salesman. Clearly, these objectives will be the logical result of breaking down the marketing objectives into actual sales targets.

All companies set themselves overall objectives which in turn imply the development of specific marketing objectives. In this chapter we have

Table 8.2   Objectives for the individual salesman

Task	The standard	How to set the standard	How to measure performance	What to look for
1 To achieve his personal sales target	Sales target per period of time for individual groups and/or products	Analysis of — territory potential — individual customers' potential Discussion and agreement between salesman and manager	Comparison of individual salesman's product sales against targets	Significant shortfall between target and achievement over a meaningful period
2 To sell the required range and quantity to individual customers	Achievement of specified range and quantity of sales to a particular customer or group of customers within an agreed time period	Analysis of individual customer records of — potential — present sales Discussion and agreement between manager and salesman	Scrutiny of — individual customer records — observation of selling in the field	Failure to achieve agreed objectives. Complacency with range of sales made to individual customers
3 To plan journeys and call frequencies to achieve minimum practicable selling cost	To achieve appropriate call frequency on individual customers. Number of live customer calls during a given time period	Analysis of individual customers' potential. Analysis of order/call ratios. Discussion and agreement between manager and salesman	Scrutiny of — individual customer records Analysis of order/call ratio. Examination of call reports	High ratio of calls to an individual customer relative to that customer's yield. Shortfall on agreed total number of calls made over an agreed time period
4 To acquire new customers	Number of prospect calls during time period. Selling new products to existing customers	Identify total number of potential and actual customers who could produce results. Identify opportunity areas for prospecting	Examination of — call reports — records of new accounts opened — ratio of existing to potential customers	Shortfall in number of prospect calls from agreed standard. Low ratio of existing to potential customers

Table 8.2 – *cont.*

Task	The standard	How to set the standard	How to measure performance	What to look for
5 To make a sales approach of the required quality	To exercise the necessary skills and techniques required to achieve the identified objective of each element of the sales approach. Continuous use of sales material	Standard to be agreed in discussion between manager and salesman related to company standards laid down	Regular observations of field selling using a systematic analysis of performance in each stage of the sales approach	Failure to — identify objective of each stage of sales approach — specific areas of skill, weakness — use of support material

discussed personal selling in the context of the overall marketing activity. This approach leads us to the following hierarchy of objectives: *corporate objectives—marketing objectives—sales objectives*, as outlined in Figure 8.1.

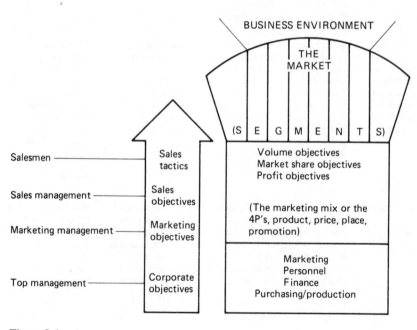

Figure 8.1

The benefits to sales force management of following this approach can be summarized as follows:

1 Co-ordination of corporate and marketing objectives with actual sales effort.
2 Establishment of a circular relationship between corporate objectives and customer wants.
3 Improvement of sales effectiveness through an understanding of the corporate and marketing implications of sales decisions.

The following example illustrates the main point that a sales force cannot be managed in isolation from broad corporate and marketing objectives. The sales force of a company manufacturing stainless steel containers was selling almost any kind of container to almost anybody who could buy. This caused severe production planning and distribution problems throughout the business, down to the purchase of raw materials. Eventually the company's profitability was seriously affected. The sales force was finally instructed to concentrate on certain kinds of products and on certain kinds of user industries. This decision eventually led to economies of scale throughout the whole organization.

To summarize, the sales force is a vital but very expensive element of the marketing mix and as much care should be devoted to its management as to any other area of marketing management. This is most likely to be achieved if intuitive sense, which is associated with experience, can be combined with the kind of logical framework of thinking outlined here (see Figure 8.2).

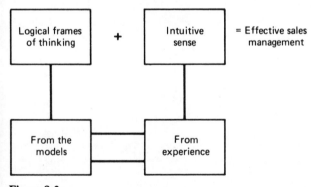

Figure 8.2

Application questions

1 What are the key functions of salesmen in your organization? How is their work co-ordinated?

2 How is the sales force deployed: by geographical territory; by product range; by type of customer? Is this deployment optimal? What other patterns of deployment should be considered by your organization?

3 Who is responsible for the sales force in your organization? What is the relationship between this post of responsibility and other marketing responsibilities in the organization? Does this cause any problems? Where problems arise, how could they be solved?

4 Can you make a case to justify the present size and type of sales force used? Could you defend your position if you were requested to cut back the sales force by 30 per cent? How would you make your case? What do you believe would be the consequences of a 30 per cent cutback in the sales force?

5 How is your own organization's sales force used? Is this the best possible use of the sales force? In what ways do activities of the sales force complement other forms of marketing communications used? Identify any other ways in which you feel the activities of the sales force could enhance the total marketing communications effort.

6 Critically appraise your company's sales plan. Does it flow naturally from the company's marketing objectives?

9 The Pricing Plan

The first important point to be made about the pricing plan is that very rarely is there a pricing plan in a marketing plan!

The reason is not too hard to find. Promotion, in all its various forms, can be managed and measured as a discrete subset of the marketing mix. So too can distribution. But while the product itself, the price charged, service elements and communication strategies are all part of the 'offer' which is made to the customer, price itself is such an integral part of the offer that it is rarely separated out and put into a plan of its own.

It is more common to find objectives for a certain group of products or for a particular group of customers, with a pricing strategy attached to it in whatever detail is necessary to indicate what the pricing policy is expected to do to help the company achieve its marketing objectives.

However, we have chosen to address the issue of pricing as a separate element of the marketing mix because this is the only sensible way that all the complex issues relating to pricing can be discussed. We shall, then, refer throughout to a pricing plan as if the intention were to write a separate pricing plan, although it will be structured in such a way that the elements of pricing can be integrated into the individual product/segment plans as appropriate.

The same could, of course, be said for each of the other elements of the marketing mix discussed in this book. How they are all integrated into a total plan is discussed in detail in Chapter 12.

Pricing and accountants

Many people know the story told on pricing courses of the conversation between the restaurateur who decides to put a peanut rack on the end of his

131

counter and his accountant expert. Essentially the plan is to sell peanuts for 10p a bag, the cost price being 6p.

Unfortunately the accountant insists that the restaurateur must allocate a proportion of overheads into the peanut operation, including rent, heat, light, equipment, depreciation, decorating, salaries, the cook's wages, window washing, soap, and so on. These allocated costs, plus a rent for the vacant amount of counter space, amount to £1563 a year which, on the basis of a sales level of fifty bags of peanuts a week, amount to 60p per bag, so demonstrating that at a selling price of 10p per bag the restaurateur would be losing 50 pence on every bag!

Many readers will appreciate the feelings of the restaurateur and will readily agree that nowhere in an organization are the seeds of potential strife more firmly sown than in the interface between accountants and marketing people, particularly when it comes to pricing issues.

Accountants often fail to understand the essential role that marketing plays in an organization. Many accountants know quite a lot about business in general, but very little about marketing, and what little is known tends to be somewhat jaundiced. Somehow marketing is seen as a less worthy activity than the act of producing goods for society. Marketing's more vocal activities, such as television advertising, are not seen in their total perspective, and it is not always easy to understand the complex decisions that have to be made about an activity that is concerned essentially with human behaviour rather than with things that can be conveniently counted. But the blame lies just as much on the side of marketers.

For their part, those marketing people who fail to understand both the financial consequences of their decisions and the constraints of money on their decision-making, have only themselves to blame for the inevitable internecine disputes that arise.

One area where it all bubbles to the surface is pricing. Our intention here is to explain pricing from a marketing point of view, while still recognizing the financial constraints and implications which accountants face. For one thing is certain. Any team comprising a financially alert marketer and a marketing-orientated accountant will make formidable opposition in any market. 'Demand exists only at a price', so price is an important determinant of how much of a certain product will sell, although it is obviously not the only factor involved. Given its importance, both as an element in the overall marketing mix, and as a major factor in determining profitability, it is somewhat surprising to find just how haphazard the pricing policy of so many companies is. More sophistication might be expected.

The pricing decision is important for two main reasons: price not only affects the margin through its impact on revenue; it also affects the quantity sold through its influence on demand. In short, price has an interactive effect on the other elements of the marketing mix, so it is essential that it is part of a conscious marketing scheme with objectives which have been clearly defined.

Although in some areas of the economy pricing may be determined by forces which are largely outside the control of corporate decision-makers, prices in the market place are normally the result of decisions made by company managements. What should the decision be, however, when on the one hand the accountant wants to increase the price of a product in order to maximize profitability, while the marketer wants to hold or even reduce the net selling price in order to increase market share? The answer would appear to be simple. Get the calculator out and see which proposal results in the biggest 'profit'.

But possibly there are some nagging doubts about the delightful simplicity of this approach. In order to introduce a structured consideration of such doubts, let us first quote in full the Boston Consulting Group on the issue of the almost defunct British motor cycle industry. 'The fundamental feature is its emphasis on model-by-model profits made. It is seen as essential that throughout the life cycle, each model, in each market where it is sold, should yield a margin of profit over the costs incurred in bringing it to the market. With this as the primary goal, a number of subsidiary policies follows:

1 Products should be up-rated or withdrawn whenever the accounting system shows they are unprofitable. Unfortunately, the accounting system will be based on existing methods of production and channels of distribution, not on cost levels that could be achieved under new systems and with different volumes.

2 Prices are set at levels necessary to achieve profitability and will be raised higher if possible.

3 The cost of an effective marketing system is only acceptable in markets where the British are already established and hence profitable. New markets will only be opened up to the extent that their development will not mean significant front end expense investment in establishing sales and distribution systems ahead of sales.

4 Plans and objectives are primarily orientated towards earning a profit on this existing business and facilities of the company, rather than on the development of a long-term position of strength in the industry.'

These are the policies that led to the British industry's low and falling share of world markets, to its progressive concentration on higher and higher displacement models. What is more, profitability, the central short-term objective to which these policies have been directed, has in fact deteriorated in the longer term to levels that now call into question the whole viability of the industry.

We now know, of course, that the British motor cycle industry is, to all intents and purposes, dead, and the above viewpoint of the Boston Consulting Group about pricing and profits must be seriously considered at least as a contributing factor. This view is echoed in the National Westminster Bank *Quarterly Review*, which stated: 'The disastrous commercial performance of the British motorcycle industry has resulted from failure to understand the strategic implications of the relationship between manufacturing volumes and the relative cost position.'

In contrast, the typical Japanese company makes dedicated efforts to increase its market share, and will often achieve this by cutting its prices, despite the possible short-term penalties of doing so. In other words there has tended to be a recognition of the pay-off in the longer term from the sacrifice of short-term profitability.

However, there remain some serious doubts even about this point of view. It is a well-known fact that manufacturers and retailers alike have begun to question the value of price cuts, especially when, against a background of falling profitability, research shows that the average housewife, far from having a precise knowledge of prices, has only a general understanding of and feeling towards value and price.

The idea of a price cut, of course, is to increase the quantity sold, as shown in Figure 9.1. The aim is for area B ($p_2 \times q_2$) to be bigger than area A ($p_1 \times q_1$). Additionally, increased volume should lead in theory to cost reductions through the experience effect (explained in Chapter 5). However, what often happens is that market sales do *not* increase enough to balance revenue and costs, with the result that profitability declines. The result is shown in Figure 9.2, area B being less than area A. It is expressed in another way in Figure 9.3.

This brings into focus the question of *time*, for the shape of demand curves changes over time, depending on a number of factors. There can be little merit in accepting profit reductions in the *long* as well as the *short* term.

It is appropriate then to begin to introduce those factors that should be taken into account when trying to resolve the question raised earlier of whether the objective for pricing should be to increase profitability or to increase market share. These factors are:

— objectives (corporate and marketing) and the product portfolio
— product life cycle
— product's position in the market
— competitors
— potential competitors
— costs (own and competitors)
— channels of distribution

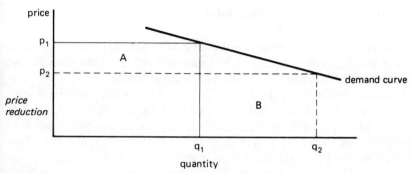

Figure 9.1

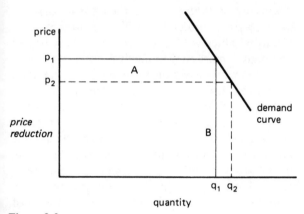

Figure 9.2

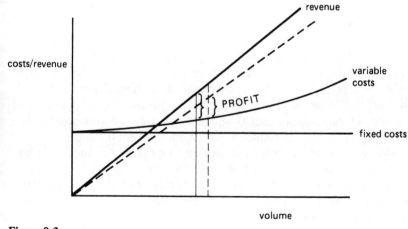

Figure 9.3

Objectives and the product portfolio

Unfortunately, many arguments within firms about pricing take place in the sort of vacuum which is created when no one has bothered to specify the *objectives* to which pricing is supposed to be contributing.

We know now that it is important that a company should have a well-defined hierarchy of objectives to which all its activities and actions, including pricing, can be related. For example, corporate objectives may well dictate that the generation of short-term profits is a requirement. (This may well be due to a particular business unit's position in a matrix *vis à vis* other units in the same corporation. For example, a group decision may have been taken to invest heavily in one business unit's growth and to fund this growth from one of their 'cash cow' units elsewhere in their portfolio.)

The point is that in reality *corporate* objectives will have an important influence on *marketing* objectives, which were discussed in detail in Chapter 5. In the same way, a company's marketing objectives for a particular product may dictate a short-term emphasis on profitability rather than market share, and this will obviously influence the pricing strategy. This will be a function of that product's position *vis à vis* other products in the portfolio. For example, it may well be that a product is one of many 'wildcats', and the company has chosen others rather than this particular one to invest in. This would naturally result in a wish to make the biggest possible contribution to profits from the product, and the pricing strategy would seek to achieve this. The setting of marketing objectives for any particular product, then, is without doubt the starting point in any consideration of pricing.

Product life cycle

The importance of the product life cycle in determining marketing objectives has already been stressed. For example, for a product estimated to be in the maturity stage of a life cycle, with only a short time to run, it would probably be unwise to set market share growth as a marketing objective. Profit contribution would probably be a more appropriate goal, providing of course market share did not slip to a point below which it would jeopardize the company's ability to introduce a new or replacement product.

On the other hand, if there is estimated to be plenty of life left in the product, it can often make a lot of sense to reduce the price in order to maintain market share. It will be remembered that when the market reaches saturation level, we could well have a very profitable 'cash cow' on our hands for many years to come.

It is also important to stress that the role of pricing will change over a product's life cycle. For example, during the high growth phase in the product life cycle, price tends not to be the customer's primary consideration, since demand is growing at such a rapid rate and it is still relatively 'new'. Here there are plenty of profit opportunities, which have to be carefully balanced against market share considerations.

It is important, then, not to write one's pricing policy on 'tablets of stone'. One large retailer's policy was to enter a market later in the product's life cycle, to price very low, and to promote heavily. However, life cycle analysis indicated to the company that it unwittingly bought some products early in the life cycle, *to which they applied exactly the same pricing strategy*. They quickly realized that they were giving profits away unnecessarily and from then on began to be more thoughtful about pricing, devising pricing policies that were appropriate to the product's progress through the life cycle.

Product positioning

The meaning of the term 'product positioning' was explained in Chapter 4. For pricing, it is a highly relevant concept. It is clearly foolish, for example, to position a product as a high-quality, exclusive item, and then to price it too low. Price is one of the clearest signals a customer has of the value of the offer that a company is making him, and there has to be a sensible relationship between the two.

Three simple examples will suffice to illustrate this point. One company launched a new pure juice product on the market after tests had indicated an overwhelming acceptance by consumers. When sales fell far short of expectations, research indicated that consumers simply did not believe that the claims on the can about the product could be true at such a low price. So the company doubled the price and re-launched it, and it was a resounding success.

Another company launched a luxury car in the 1960s and priced it on its standard cost-plus basis. Customers were buying the car and re-selling it immediately at a much inflated price. In other words, the *value* of the car to the customer was much greater than the actual price charged.

Likewise, some tertiary educational establishments claim their courses are the best in the world, then charge lower prices than their competitors. Research indicates that for directors and very senior managers in industry, a low price is more likely to be counter-productive because in this particular product field it is considered to be an indicator of quality.

Product positioning, then, is another major consideration in the pricing decision.

Competition and potential competition

In spite of product positioning, most products have competitors, and it goes without saying that these must be carefully considered.

It is true, of course, that what are referred to derisively as 'pimply little me-too products' cannot in most circumstances be expected to succeed if they are higher priced than competitive products. It is also true in such circumstances, that if price is a principal determinant of demand, being higher priced is unlikely to be the right strategy.

This brings into sharp focus again the whole question of product positioning and market segmentation. It will be clear that wherever possible a company should be seeking to blend the ingredients of the marketing mix in such a way that their 'offer' to the customer cannot be compared directly with anyone else's 'offer'. For if two offers *can* be directly compared, it is obvious that the one with the lowest price will win most of the time.

Nonetheless, competitive products, in all their forms, clearly have to be taken into account in the pricing decision, as indeed do *potential* competitors.

Some firms launch new products at high prices to recover their investment costs, only to find that they have provided a price 'umbrella' to entice competitors, who then launch similar products at much lower prices, thus moving down the experience curve quicker, often taking the originator's market away from him in the process. A lower launch price, with possibly a quicker rate of diffusion and hence a greater rate of experience, may make it more difficult for a potential competitor to enter the market profitably.

Costs

Another key factor for consideration is costs—not just our own costs, but those of our competitors as well. There are many cost concepts, and this is not the right medium to go into any detail. However, the two most common cost concepts are *marginal costing* and *full absorption costing*.

The conventional profit-maximizing model of economists tends to indicate that a price should be set at the point where marginal cost equals marginal revenue, i.e. where the additional cost of producing and marketing an additional unit is equivalent to the additional revenue earned from its sale. The theory is indisputable, but in practice this procedure is difficult if not impossible to apply. This is largely because the economists' model assumes that price is the only determinant of demand, whereas in reality this is not always so.

In practice, the costs of manufacturing (or provision of a service) provide the basis for most pricing decisions, i.e. a 'cost-plus' method. However, as the example given earlier indicates, the trouble with most such 'cost-oriented' pricing approaches is that they make little attempt to reconcile what the customer is prepared to pay with what it costs the company to be in business and make a fair return on its investment of resources.

An example of the 'cost-oriented' approach is when a company targets for a certain return on costs, i.e. the company will set itself a target level of profits at a certain projected level of sales volume. In fact, this type of approach uses a simple form of 'break-even' analysis as depicted in Figure 9.4.

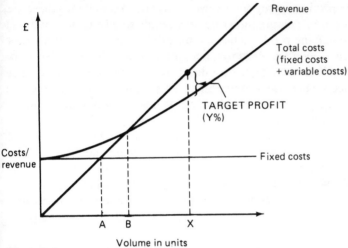

Figure 9.4

In the diagram, fixed costs are shown as a straight line and all other costs are allocated on a cost-per-unit basis to produce an ascending curve. At point A, revenue covers only fixed costs. At point B, all costs are covered and any additional sales will produce net profit. At point X, Y% target profit is being achieved. Obviously, the major problem with such an approach to pricing is that it tends to assume that at a given price a given number of products will be sold, whereas in reality, the quantity sold is bound to be dependent to a certain extent on the price charged. Also, this model assumes a break-even *point*, whereas in most companies the best that can be said is that there is a break-even *area* at a given level of production. It is however, quite useful for helping us to understand the relationship between different kinds of costs.

By far the most common way of setting price is to use the cost-plus approach, arriving at a price which yields margins commensurate with declared profit objectives.

When making a pricing decision, it is wise to consider a number of different costing options, for any one can be misleading on its own, particularly those that allocate fixed costs to all products in the portfolio. Often the basis of allocation is debatable, and an unthinking marketer may well accept the costs as given and easily make the wrong pricing decision.

For example, in difficult economic times, when cost savings are sought, unprofitable products are eliminated from the range. Unprofitable products are identified by the gross or net margins in the last complete trading year, and also by estimates of these margins against estimated future sales. However, because conventional cost accounting allocates the highest costs to high-volume products, they show lower margins, so sometimes these are sacrificed. But product elimination often saves only small amounts of direct costs, so the remaining products have to absorb higher costs, and the next profitability crisis appears. Product elimination also reduces the scale of operations, as well as reducing the product mix, so there is less incentive to invest and the company is less competitive. This approach may be repeated several times under successive management teams and sometimes leads to the demise of the company.

The writer has coined the expression *'anorexia industrialosa'* for this process, which describes an excessive desire to be leaner and fitter, leading to total emaciation and eventually death!

This is not intended to be an attack on any kind of total average costing method. Our intention here is merely to advise caution and a broader perspective when using any kind of costing system as a basis for pricing decisions.

Finally, some account has to be taken of our competitors' costs and to try to understand the basis of his pricing policies. For clearly, everything that has been said so far about pricing applies as much to him as it does to us.

Whatever your pricing problem, however, you will never go far wrong if you sit alongside your accountant and discuss all these issues with him.

Channels of distribution

Conventional pricing theory does not help much in determining one's policy towards distributor margins. The intermediaries which constitute a particular marketing channel perform a number of functions on behalf of the supplier which enables the exchange transaction between producer and consumer to be fulfilled. In return for their services, these intermediaries seek to be rewarded; this reward is in effect the 'margin' between the price of the goods ex the factory, and the price the consumer pays. However, the total channel margin may have to be shared between several intermediaries and still reach the consumer at a competitive price. Intermediaries therefore live or die on the economics of their respective operations. The ideal reward structure in the marketing channel is to ensure that an acceptable rate of return on investment is earned at each level; this situation is often not achieved because of the imbalances of bargaining power present.

There are a number of devices available for rewarding channel intermediaries, most of which take the form of discounts against a nominal price list. These are:

Trade discount	This is discount given against the price list for services made available by the intermediary, e.g. holding inventory, buying in bulk, redistribution, etc.
Quantity discount	A quantity discount is offered to intermediaries who order in large lots.
Promotional discount	This is the discount given to distributors to encourage them to share jointly in the promotion of the product(s) involved.
Cash discount	In order to encourage prompt payments of accounts, a cash discount of around 2½ per cent for payment within 10 days is often offered.

In the situation where there is a dynamic marketing channel, there will be constant pressure upon suppliers to improve margins. Because of these pressures the question of margins should be seen at a strategic as well as a tactical level. This whole area of margin management can be viewed as a series of trade-off type decisions which determine how the total channel margin should be split. The concept of the total channel margin is simple. It is the difference between the level of price at which we wish to position our product in the ultimate market place and the cost of our product at the factory gate. Who takes what proportion of this difference is what margin management is about. The problem is shown in Figure 9.5.

It will be seen that the firm's channel requirements will only be achieved if it either carries them out itself or if it goes some way towards meeting the requirements of an intermediary who can perform those functions on its behalf. The objective of the firm in this respect could therefore be expressed in terms of willingness to trade off margin in order to achieve its marketing goals. Such a trade-off need not lead to a loss of profitability; indeed as Figure 9.6 suggests, the margin is only one element in the determination of profitability, profitability being defined as the rate of return on net worth (net worth being share capital and capital reserves plus retained profits).

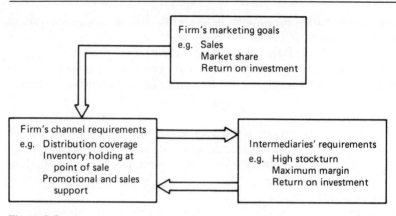

Figure 9.5

It can be seen that by improving the utilization of capital assets (capital management) as well as by using a higher gearing, it is possible to operate successfully on lower margins if this means that marketing goals can be achieved more effectively.

From the foregoing it becomes apparent that the question of margins (both the margin retained by the firm and thus by implication the margin allowed the distributor) cannot be examined without consideration of the wider implications of overall marketing strategy and the financial policy and capital structure of the firm.

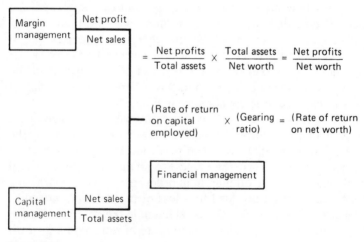

Figure 9.6

Preparing the pricing plan

We have so far considered some of the main issues relevant to the pricing decision. We can now try to pull all of these issues together. However, let us first recapitulate on one of the basic findings which underpin the work of the Boston Consulting Group.

It will be recalled that, under certain circumstances, real costs reduce with accumulated experience. Figure 9.7 describes this effect. One of the implica-

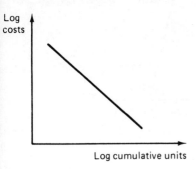

Figure 9.7

tions of this is that unless a firm accumulates experience at the same or at a greater rate than the market as a whole, eventually its costs will become uncompetitive. Figure 9.8 illustrates this point.

There is a large range of pricing policies. However, many of these can be simplified into what is referred to either as a *skimming* policy or a *penetration*

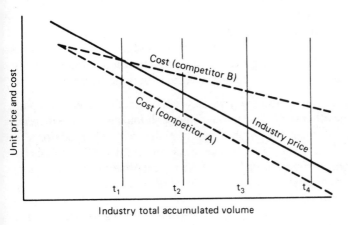

t = time period

Figure 9.8

policy. It is easiest to consider these policies in the context of new product launches. Essentially a skimming policy is a high initial price, moving down the experience curve at a slower rate, while a penetration policy is a low initial price, with a much faster rate of product adoption, hence a steeper experience curve. Both policies are summarized in Figure 9.9a and b.

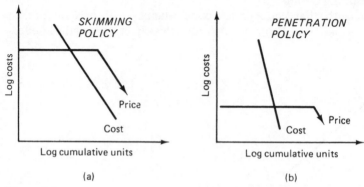

Figure 9.9

The circumstances favouring a skimming policy are:

1 Demand is likely to be price inelastic.
2 There are likely to be different price-market segments, thereby appealing to those buyers first who have a higher range of acceptable prices.
3 Little is known about the costs of producing and marketing the product.

The circumstances favouring a penetration policy are:

1 Demand is likely to be price elastic.
2 Competitors are likely to enter the market quickly.
3 There are no distinct and separate price-market segments.
4 There is the possibility of large savings in production and marketing costs if a large sales volume can be generated (the experience factor).

However, great caution is necessary whatever the circumstances and apart from these, all the other factors mentioned above should also be considered.

In conclusion, it must be emphasized that the price charged for the product affects and is affected by the other elements of the marketing mix. It is a common mistake to assume either that the lowest price will get the order, or that we can sell enough of our product at a cost-plus price to give us the required rate of return.

The reality is that pricing policy should be determined after account has been taken of all factors which impinge on the pricing decision. These are summarized in Figure 9.10. The first shows the discretionary pricing range

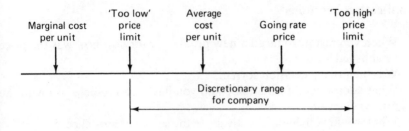

Pricing alternatives for a hypothetical company

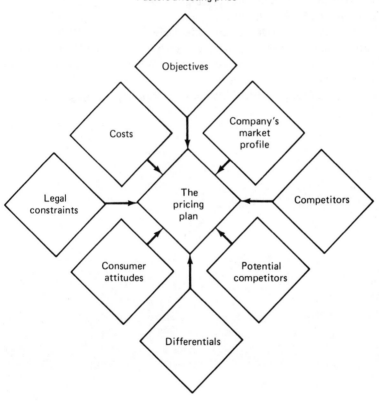

Factors affecting price

Figure 9.10

for a company. The second shows those factors we should take account of in reaching a pricing decision.

Application questions

1 When you last introduced a new product or service, how was the price established?
Was the pricing decision correct?
What additional information could you have used to help you with the pricing decision?
What would you do differently given the same circumstances?
2 Describe your pricing strategy for one of your major products. How does it compare with that of your major competitors?
3 Describe how you deal with pricing
(a) in times of high inflation
(b) at each phase in the product life cycle
4 During the past ten years, what trends have occurred in margins in your industry? Are these trends acceptable? What policy has your organization got towards these trends?
5 Are trade margins justified? What is your policy towards trade margins?

10 The Distribution Plan

Some readers, alas, will not even bother to read this chapter, because distribution is perceived as outside the scope of marketing. They would, in common with many businesses, tend to think only of physical distribution, or the transportation of goods, rather than of what distribution is really about. In this chapter we show why distribution is very much the concern of marketers, and what should go into a distribution plan.

The topic of product distribution involves three main decision areas, each of which will be examined in turn:

1 How is the physical movement of our product organized?
2 Through what marketing channels do we reach our customers (or what channels do our customers utilize to acquire our products)?
3 What level of availability of our product does our customer require (and how well do we meet this requirement)?

Physical distribution

The physical distribution function of a firm provides the place and time dimensions which constitute the third element of the marketing mix. This is depicted in Figure 10.1, which also shows its relationship to the other utility-producing elements. The figures on the diagram are illustrative only, although they are realistic for some industries.

If a product is not available when and where the customer wants it, it will surely fail in the market. To achieve this value-adding function, firms generally have a distributive activity within the corporate organizational structure known variously as physical distribution management (PDM), traffic management, marketing logistics, or simply, logistics. A generalized

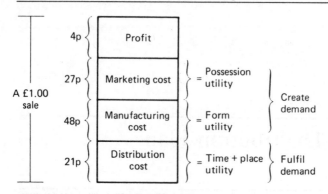

Figure 10.1

model of the entire corporate entity is given in Figure 10.2; this also depicts the position of (finished) product distribution *vis-à-vis* marketing, production, the procurement system, and the financial/accounting systems.

The movement of all materials, both prior to production (raw materials, sub-assemblies, etc) and after production (finished product) constitutes the total logistics flow of the firm. In this chapter, however, we shall confine our attention to the latter, i.e. finished product distribution.

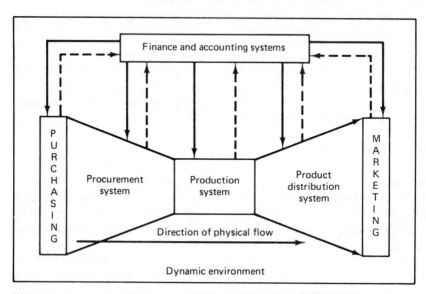

Key: ▬ ▬ ▬ ▬ Feedback

Figure 10.2

The distribution mix

In a typical manufacturing company without a formal distribution structure, the responsibility for distribution-related matters is spread across the other functional departments. For example, production may control warehousing and transportation; marketing may control the channels through which the product moves, the levels of service provided to the customer, and inventory obsolescence; and the finance department may control communications, data processing, and inventory costs. Such a compartmentalized arrangement leads to each department working to its own objectives, attempting to optimize its own particular activity oblivious of others or the good of the whole company. Introducing a more formalized distribution arrangement into the corporate organizational structure, although not completely eliminating interdepartmental friction, does at least ensure that all distribution-related activities are organized under a more centralized control, thereby gaining focus.

This then is the basis of the total distribution concept, because it now becomes possible to seek out potential 'trade-offs', i.e. consciously to incur costs in one area in order to achieve an even larger benefit in another. For example, should a series of field warehouses be maintained, or would one suffice, supplemented by an improved trucking operation? Of course, these types of potential 'trade-off' situations place a heavy burden on the cost-reporting systems of a company.

The professional distribution manager, therefore, has several variables to contend with in his search for trade-offs; taken together these constitute the *distribution mix*. Each of these will now be examined briefly.

FACILITIES

Decisions in this area are concerned with the problem of how many warehouses and plants should be established and where they should be located. Obviously for the majority of companies it is necessary to take the location of existing plants and warehouses as given in the short term, but the question does arise in the longer term or indeed when new plants or warehouses are being considered.

The principal marketing task here is to forecast the nature, size and geographical spread of demand. Increasing the number of field locations will result in an increase in trucking costs and a reduction in retail distribution costs. So another marketing task is to determine the customer service levels that are likely to be required in order to be able to make a decision about this particular trade-off.

INVENTORY

A major element in any company's total distribution costs is the cost of holding stock which is often as high as 30 per cent of its value per annum. This is because of items such as interest charges, deterioration, shrinkage, insurance, administration, and so on. Thus decisions about how much inventory to hold, where to hold it, in what quantities to order, and so on, are vital issues. Inventory levels are also instrumental in determining the level of service that the company offers the customer.

TRANSPORT

The important aspects of the transport decision concern such issues as what mode of transport should be used, whether to own vehicles or lease them, how to schedule deliveries, how often to deliver, and so on. Perhaps of the five distribution variables, it is transport that receives the greatest attention within the firm. It is certainly one of the more obvious facets of the distribution task.

COMMUNICATIONS

It must always be remembered that distribution not only involves the flow of materials through the distribution channel, but also the flow of information. Here we are talking about the order processing system, the invoicing system, the demand forecasting system, and so on. Without effective communications support, the distribution system will never be capable of providing satisfactory customer service at an acceptable cost. It is vital that it should be recognized that inefficiency here can lead to a build-up of costs in other areas of the business, such as, for example, in emergency deliveries as well as a permanent loss of sales through customers turning to alternative sources of supply.

UNITIZATION

The way in which goods are packaged and then subsequently accumulated into larger unit sizes (e.g. a pallet-load) can have a major bearing upon distribution economics. For example, the ability to stack goods on a pallet which then becomes the unit load for movement and storage can lead to considerable cost savings in terms of handling and warehousing. Similarly the use of containers as the basic unit of movement has revolutionized international transport and, to a certain extent, domestic transport as well. Mobile racking systems and front-end pricing by means of scanners are other unitization innovations that have had a dramatic effect upon the way goods are marketed.

Together, these five areas constitute the total cost of distribution within a company.

Marketing channels

The fundamental role of a company's distribution function is to ensure that the 'right product is available at the right time'. This implies some organization of resources into channels through which the product moves to customers. A marketing channel may therefore be considered as the course taken in the transfer of the title of a commodity (which in turn may be either a product or service) from its original source of supply to its ultimate consumption. It is necessary to consider both the route of exchange (and its administrative and financial control), and the physical movement route of the product—they may well be different. Many companies use multiple

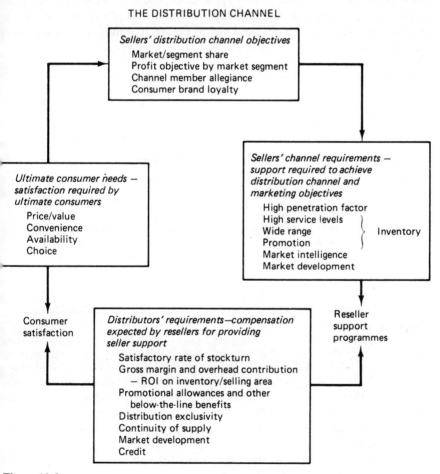

THE DISTRIBUTION CHANNEL

Sellers' distribution channel objectives
Market/segment share
Profit objective by market segment
Channel member allegiance
Consumer brand loyalty

*Ultimate consumer needs —
satisfaction required by
ultimate consumers*
Price/value
Convenience
Availability
Choice

*Sellers' channel requirements —
support required to achieve
distribution channel and
marketing objectives*
High penetration factor
High service levels ⎫
Wide range ⎬ Inventory
Promotion ⎭
Market intelligence
Market development

Consumer
satisfaction

*Distributors' requirements—compensation
expected by resellers for providing
seller support*
Satisfactory rate of stockturn
Gross margin and overhead contribution
— ROI on inventory/selling area
Promotional allowances and other
below-the-line benefits
Distribution exclusivity
Continuity of supply
Market development
Credit

Reseller
support
programmes

Figure 10.3

marketing channels through which to reach their customers, often involving one or even several 'intermediaries'. The role of an intermediary is to provide the means of achieving the widest possible market coverage at a lower unit cost. Many intermediaries hold stock and thereby share some of the financial risk with the principal (or supplier). Figure 10.3 shows that using an intermediary carries benefits for the manufacturer, but it also involves significant 'costs', the most important of which is the loss of control which accompanies such a channel strategy.

Often too, considerable conflict exists between the respective objectives of the supplier and his distributors; this gives rise to conflict and suspicion in the relationship. Nevertheless, a supplier must evaluate the costs and benefits of each marketing channel potentially open to him and decide on a combination which best suits his type of business and the markets he is engaged in. The alternatives depicted in Figure 10.4 quite obviously have different cost/revenue profiles.

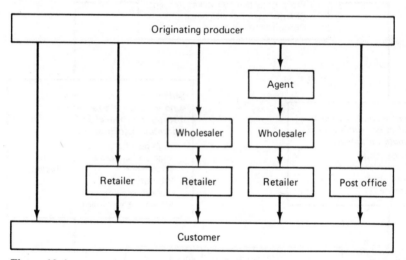

Figure 10.4

Any cost/benefit appraisal needs to be undertaken in the widest context possible. It needs to consider questions of market strategy, the appropriateness of the channel to the product, and customer requirements, as well as the question of the comparative costs of selling and distribution.

Marketing channel decisions are therefore key decisions which involve the choice of an intermediary (or intermediaries) and detailed consideration of the physical distribution implications of all the alternatives. The evaluation of intermediaries is therefore of significant importance.

EVALUATION CRITERIA FOR CHANNEL INTERMEDIARIES

Regardless of the type of middlemen to be used, there are a number of basic evaluation criteria, for example:

Does he now, or will he, sell to our target market segment?
Is his sales force large enough and trained well enough to achieve our regional sales forecasts?
Is his regional location adequate in respect of the retail (and other) outlets serviced?
Are his promotional policies and budgets adequate?
Does he satisfy customer after-sales requirements?
Are his product policies consistent with our own?
Does he carry competitive lines?
What are his inventory policies regarding width, depth and cover?
Is he credit worthy?
Is distributor management receptive, aggressive, and flexible?

All the above factors, and others, have to be considered when making specific decisions on choice of intermediaries, which in turn is part of the overall channel selection issue.

Customer service

Quite simply, the output of a firm's distribution activities is the provision of product availability to meet customer demands, i.e. *customer service.* Increasingly, it is customer service above all else (including price) which is being sought by purchasers of goods and services.

However, the provision of customer service in all its various forms is likely to involve the firm in large financial commitments. In fact it can be demonstrated that once the level of service (defined here as the percentage of occasions the product is available to the customer, when and where he wants it) increases beyond the 70–80 per cent mark, the associated costs increase exponentially. Figure 10.5 demonstrates the typical relationship between the level of availability and the cost of providing it. From this diagram it will be observed that the cost of increasing the service level by a small amount, say from 95 per cent to 97.5 per cent, results in a sharp increase in inventory costs.

The implications of this cost relationship bear closer examination. Significantly, many companies appear to be unaware of the level of service they are offering, i.e. there is *no* customer service policy as such. Even where such a policy does exist, the levels are quite often arbitrarily set and are not the result of a careful market analysis. The question then arises: what level of availability *should* be offered? This question is relatively simple to answer in

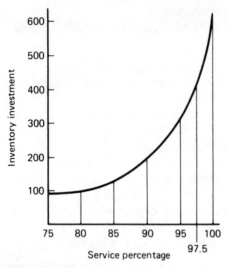

Figure 10.5

theory, very difficult to quantify and achieve in practice, since different product groups in different market segments could well demand different levels of customer service.

In theory at least it is possible to say that service levels can continue to be improved as long as the marketing advantage that results continues to outrun the additional costs incurred. Conceptually it is possible to draw an S-shaped curve (see Figure 10.6) which suggests that at very high levels of customer service, customers are unable to distinguish between small changes in the service offered. When a company is operating in this region, it is quite possibly incurring more costs than are necessary for the level of sales being achieved.

For example, marketing and sales managers who insist on offering maximum service to all customers, no matter what the profitability and

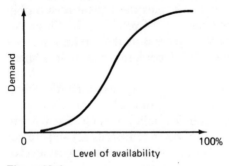

Figure 10.6

location of those customers, are quite probably doing their company a disservice. By carefully reviewing customer service policy, perhaps even introducing differential service levels for different products or for different customers (at least on a trial-and-error basis) marketing can enhance its contribution to corporate profitability.

Somewhere between the costs and benefits involved in customer service, a balance has to be found. It will be at that point where the additional revenue returns for each increment of service are equal to the extra cost involved in providing that increment. To attempt to ascertain this point of balance, certain information is required, for example:

1 How profitable is the product? What contribution to fixed costs and profits does this product make and what is its sales turnover?
2 What is the nature of the product? Is it a critical item as far as the customer is concerned where stock-outs at the point of supply would result in a loss of sales? Does the product have characteristics that result in high stockholding costs?
3 What is the nature of the market? Does the company operate in a sellers' or a buyers' market? How frequently is the product purchased? Are there ready substitutes? What are the stockholding practices of the purchasers? Which markets and customers are growing and which are declining?
4 What is the nature of the competition? How many companies are providing an alternative source of supply to our customers? What sort of service levels do they offer?
5 What is the nature of the channel of distribution through which the company sells? Does the company sell direct to the end-customer, or through intermediaries? To what extent does the company control the channel and the activities of its members, such as the stock levels and order policies?

This basic information is the raw material of the service level decision. To take an example, the level of service offered is less likely to have an effect on sales if in fact the company is the sole supplier of the product, and there are no substitutes. This situation is the case in some industrial markets and from a short-term point of view to offer a higher level of service, say 90 per cent instead of 85 per cent, would probably have the effect of reducing the total profitability of the product.

Developing a customer service package

In general terms, customer service is normally defined as the service provided to the customer from the time an order is placed until the product is delivered. In fact, it is much more than this. It actually encompasses every aspect of the relationship between a manufacturer and his distributors/ customers. Under this definition, price, sales representation, after-sales service, product range offering, product availability, etc., are all dimensions of customer service, i.e. the total activity of servicing one's customer.

However, it is more traditional to think of customer service in distribution-related terms. Under this more restricted definition the key elements of customer service are product availability, overall order cycle time, and order cycle time variation. Research has shown that many companies have poor product availability due to a variety of reasons, e.g. poor forecasting, production difficulties, inadequate inventory controls, etc.

Above all else it is fundamental for suppliers to derive and make operational their concept of customer service from a study of their customers' real needs rather than their own perceptions of such needs. The following list contains the major components of customer service that should be researched.

Frequency of delivery
Time from order to delivery
Reliability of delivery
Emergency deliveries when required
Stock availability and continuity of supply
Orders filled completely
Advice on non-availability
Convenience of placing order
Acknowledgement of order
Accuracy of invoices
Quality of sales representation
Regular calls by sales representatives
Manufacturer monitoring of retail stock levels
Credit terms offered
Customer query handling
Quality of outer packaging
Well-stacked pallets
Easy-to-read use-by dates on outers
Quality of inner package for in-store handling and display
Consults on new product/package development
Reviews product range regularly
Co-ordination between production, distribution and marketing

This will almost certainly mean designing different customer service packages for different market groups. At present very few manufacturers/ suppliers bother to do this. Basically six steps are involved in this process:

1 Define the important service elements (and sub-elements).
2 Determine customers' viewpoints on these.
3 Design a competitive package (and several variations, if necessary).
4 Develop a promotional campaign to 'sell' the service package idea.
5 Pilot test a particular package and the promotional campaign being used.
6 Establish controls to monitor performance of the various service packages.

Throughout many types of industry, and especially those that are highly competitive, it is increasingly being recognized that, after all the other terms of trade have been tried and exhausted, it will be customer service considerations which will determine who in the end gets the order. The distribution function is becoming as important as that.

Developing the distribution plan

Figure 10.7 shows the interrelationship between the process described elsewhere in this book and distribution. Here we see that product, pricing and promotion decisions are separated from distribution.

Organizationally, it makes a lot of sense to make marketing responsible for distribution, since it is probably in the best position to make the difficult trade-off between very high levels of customer service and the high inventory-carrying costs associated with such levels.

On the other hand, labour relations, wage bargaining, the technical aspects, and so on, of distribution also demand specialist attention, and there is a grave danger that such issues may begin to divert too much of the chief marketing officer's attention away from other important marketing areas. The Logistics Director is one possible answer to this problem. His role is to view the whole distribution system in an integrated way.

What is integrated distribution management?

Integrated distribution management is an approach to the distribution mission of the firm whereby two or more of the functions involved in moving goods from source to user are integrated and viewed as an interrelated system or subsystem for purposes of managerial planning, implementation and control. Whatever the organizational solution, however, all of the above issues are relevant and it is necessary to know where to start.

Where to start?

The distribution audit was referred to in Chapter 2. Like the more general marketing audit referred to there, this is in two major parts—*internal* and

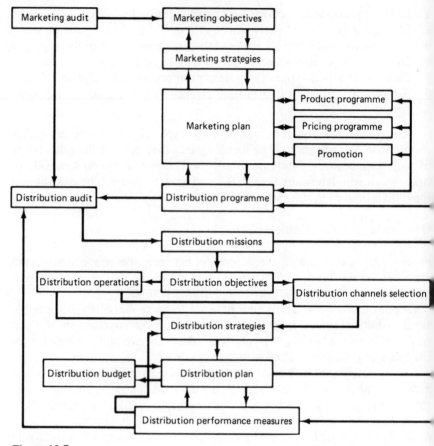

Figure 10.7

external. Figure 10.8a and b illustrates the major components of the distribution audit.

Distribution objectives can be many and varied, but the following are considered basic for marketing purposes:

1 Outlet penetration by type of distribution
2 Inventory range and levels to be held
3 Distributor sales and sales promotion activities
4 Other specific customer development programmes, e.g. incentives for distributors

When taking an integrated distribution management approach, it is as well to remember that there are a number of other decisions/trade-offs which need to be specified in the plan. These are depicted in Figure 10.9.

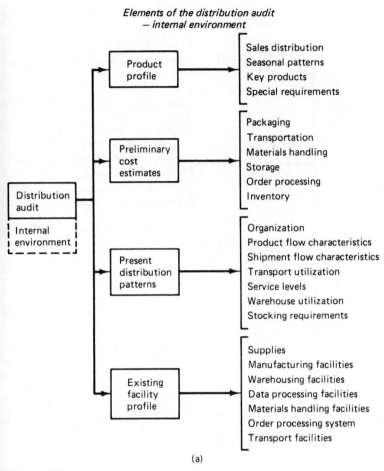

Elements of the distribution audit
– internal environment

Product
profile
- Sales distribution
- Seasonal patterns
- Key products
- Special requirements

Preliminary
cost
estimates
- Packaging
- Transportation
- Materials handling
- Storage
- Order processing
- Inventory

Distribution
audit

Internal
environment

Present
distribution
patterns
- Organization
- Product flow characteristics
- Shipment flow characteristics
- Transport utilization
- Service levels
- Warehouse utilization
- Stocking requirements

Existing
facility
profile
- Supplies
- Manufacturing facilities
- Warehousing facilities
- Data processing facilities
- Materials handling facilities
- Order processing system
- Transport facilities

(a)

Figure 10.8a

Of course all of these decisions need not necessarily be located in one plan or be made by one person or department, but clearly they need to be made and written down somewhere in the company's plans.

Finally, the following illustrates a simple iterative approach to distribution planning that should help tighten up what is often a neglected area of marketing management.

Distribution planning approach

1 Determine marketing objectives.
2 Evaluate changing conditions in distribution at all levels.
3 Determine distribution task within overall marketing strategy.

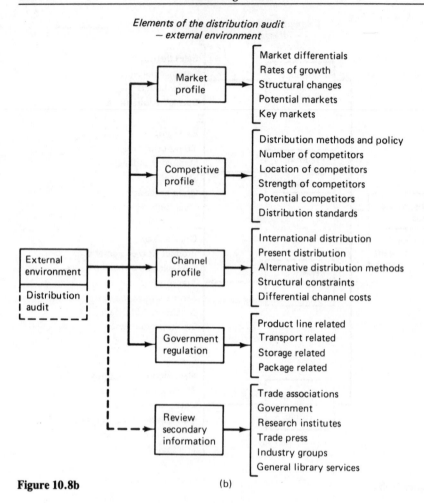

Elements of the distribution audit
— external environment

Figure 10.8b   (b)

4 Determine distribution policy in terms of type, number and level of outlets to be used.
5 Set performance standards for the distribution organization.
6 Obtain performance information.
7 Compare actual with anticipated performance.
8 Adjustment where necessary.

Application questions

1 What are the advantages and disadvantages of the channels currently used by your company?

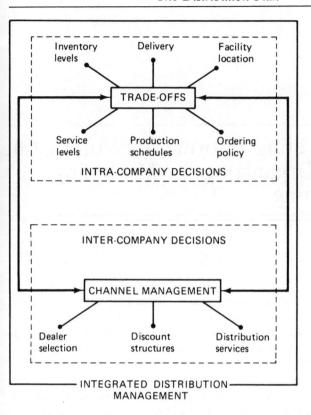

Figure 10.9

2 Are there any cases where the channels used may not be the most appropriate?

3 If your company were new to the market, what channels would you use? How would your recommendations differ from existing arrangements? What prevents you from making these changes?

4 Is logistics adequately represented at board or senior management level in your organization? How could improvements be made?

5 What coordination takes place between physical distribution management and marketing management? How can any problems be minimized?

6 How are decisions currently made concerning customer service levels? How does it compare with competitors?

7 Can you see any way of making savings in your distribution system without reducing customer service?

11 Marketing Information Forecasting and Organizing for Marketing Planning

In the next chapter we look at one of the most difficult aspects of marketing planning—actually making it all work in practice by means of a system within the company. This is something that most courses and books somehow seem to overlook. Yet no work on marketing planning can be complete without a fairly detailed consideration of how all the structures and frameworks presented in earlier chapters are to be implemented.

The truth is, of course, that the actual *process* of marketing planning is simple in outline. Any book will tell us that it consists of: a situation review; assumptions; objectives; strategies; programmes; and measurement and review. What other books *do not* tell us is that there are a number of contextual issues that have to be considered that make marketing planning one of the most baffling of all marketing problems.

Here are some of those issues:

When should it be done, *how often*, *by whom*, and *how*?
Is it different in a *large* and a *small* company?
Is it different in a *diversified* and an *undiversified* company?
Is it different in an *international* and a *domestic* company?
What is the role of the *chief executive*?
What is the role of the *planning department*?
Should marketing planning be *top down* or *bottom up*?
What is the relationship between *operational* (one year) and *strategic* (longer term) planning?

Until issues such as these are understood, the other chapters in this book will remain little more than interesting aspects of marketing planning. So the purpose of the final chapter is to help us to pick up all the pieces of the jigsaw puzzle and put them together to form a picture we can all see and understand.

First, however, we need to set the scene, and in particular to fill in a few gaps concerning marketing information, and the organizational side of marketing. Our research at Cranfield has shown very clearly that it is important to recognize at the outset what the realistic constraints are likely to be on the implementation of a marketing planning system. Two such major constraints are marketing information and a company's organizational form, which are considered in this chapter. We will then go on in the next chapter to demonstrate how marketing planning can be made to work by means of a system, and will include in this a discussion of the role of the chief executive, and the planning department. Finally, there will be a glossary of marketing planning terms.

This chapter, then, is in two parts:

1 Marketing information and forecasting
2 Marketing organization

In the final chapter we consider marketing planning systems design and implementation.

Marketing information and forecasting for marketing planning

It will by now be obvious that without information it is going to be difficult to do many of the fairly commonsense things we have been discussing so far. Any plan can only be as good as the information on which it is based, which is why we have been making sure that we know the right questions to ask, such as: 'Who are our customers?' 'What is our market share?' and so on. Throughout this book we have been stressing that the profitable development of a company can only come from a continual attempt to match the company's capabilities with customer needs. In order that the company can be sure that this matching process is taking place effectively, it is necessary that some type of information flow be instituted between the customer and the firm. This is the role of marketing research.

Difference between market research and marketing research

Put very simply, market research is concerned specifically with research about markets, whereas marketing research is concerned with research into marketing processes. We are concerned here with marketing research, which has been defined by the American Marketing Association as the systematic gathering, recording and analysis of data about problems relating to the marketing of goods and services.

The words in this definition are important. The process has to be systematic because it is necessary to have a structured interaction between people, machines and procedures designed to generate an orderly flow of pertinent information collected from sources both inside and outside the company, for use as the bases for decision-making in specified responsibility areas of marketing management.

It will be apparent immediately that data by themselves (such as words, figures, pictures, sounds, and so on) are of little use until they are combined with direction and hence become information. But without some purpose in mind, some marketing problem to solve, information is not much use either. Indeed, research has shown that one of the biggest problems facing management today is a *surplus* of data and information, rather than too little. Which brings us to our definition of *intelligence*, which is information consumable and usable by management in converting uncertainty into risk.

Uncertainty, of course, is when any outcome is considered to be equally possible. When a probability can be assigned to certain outcomes, however, we are talking about *risk*, which is just quantified uncertainty. The marketing manager might feel, for example, that a new product has a 90 per cent chance of achieving 30 per cent market share in its first year. Clearly, our ability to make successful decisions is enhanced if we are operating under conditions of known risk rather than uncertainty.

Conversion of uncertainty into risk and the minimization of risk is perhaps marketing management's most important task, and in this process the role of marketing research is of paramount importance.

How much to spend on marketing research

Before looking at the different kinds of research available to the marketing manager, a book written about marketing planning should surely address the issue of the marketing research budget.

Marketing information has to be produced, stored and distributed, but it has a limited life—it is perishable. Like other resources, information has a value in use; the less the manager knows about a marketing problem and the greater the risk attached to a wrong decision, the more valuable the information becomes. This implies the need for a cost/benefit appraisal of all sources of marketing information, since there is little point in investing more in such information than the return on it would justify. But while costs are easy to identify, the benefits are more difficult to pin down. They can best be expressed in terms of the additional profits that might be achieved through identifying marketing opportunities and through the avoidance of marketing failures that could result without the use of information.

It must be stressed, however, that the decision about how much to spend on marketing information is not an easy one. On the one hand it would generally speaking be foolhardy to proceed without any information at all, while on the other hand the cost of perfect information would be prohibitive. One way of estimating how much to spend is based on the theory of probability and expected value. For example, if by launching a product you had to incur development costs of £1 million and you believed there was a 10 per cent chance that the product would fail, the maximum *loss expectation* would be £100,000 (i.e. £1 million × 0.1).

Obviously, then, it is worth spending up to £100,000 to acquire information that would help avoid such a loss. However, because perfect information is seldom available, it makes sense to budget a small sum for marketing research which effectively discounts the likely inaccuracy of the information. Such an approach can be a valuable means of quantifying the value of marketing research in a managerial context.

Forms of marketing research

Increasing sophistication in the use of the techniques available to the researcher, particularly in the handling and analysis of multivariate data, has made marketing research into a specialized function within the field of marketing management. Nevertheless, any company, irrespective of whether or not it has a marketing department, should be aware of some of the tools that are available and where these may be used.

Marketing research can be classified either as *external* or *internal*. The former research activity is conducted within the competitive environment outside the firm, whereas much valuable intelligence can be gained from internal marketing analysis in the form of sales trends, changes in the marketing mix such as price, advertising levels, and so on. External marketing information gathering should always be seen as a complement to such internal information.

Apart from this, there is another basic split between *reactive* and *non-reactive* marketing research. Non-reactive methods are based upon the interpretation of observed phenomena or extant data, whereas reactive research involves some form of proactive assessment in the market place.

The most widely used method of reactive marketing research involves the asking of questions by means of a *questionnaire* survey, which is indeed a ubiquitous and highly flexible instrument. It can be administered by an interviewer, by telephone, or it can be sent by mail, and so on.

All of these different methods have their advantages and disadvantages, and all have different cost consequences. For example, the greatest degree of control over the quality of the responses is obtained by getting a researcher to administer each questionnaire personally, but this is very expensive and time-consuming. Telephone interviews are quick and relatively inexpensive but there is a severe limit to the amount of technical information that can be obtained by this means. The postal questionnaire is a much-favoured method, but here great care is necessary to avoid sample bias. For example, is there something special (and possibly therefore unrepresentative of the population) about those who reply to a postal questionnaire?

But without doubt the biggest potential pitfalls with the questionnaire lies in its design. Everyone knows about the 'loaded' question or the dangers of ambiguity, yet these are not always easily detectable. Indeed, even the order in which questions are asked can have a distortion effect on the answers.

Such pitfalls can be reduced by *pilot testing* it; in other words, by giving it a trial run on a sub-group of the intended sample to isolate any problems that may arise.

Sometimes it may be more appropriate to gather information not by large surveys, but by smaller-scale, more detailed studies intended to provide qualitative insights rather than quantitative conclusions. *Depth interviews* can provide such insights. These are loosely-structured discussions with a group broadly representing the population in which the researcher is interested, in which a group leader attempts to draw from the group their feelings about the subject under discussion. Such in-depth interviews can also take place with individuals, a method which is particularly popular when information is required about specialized products or markets.

Experimentation is another type of reactive marketing research which can provide a valuable source of information about the likely market perform- ance of new products or about the likely effects of variations in the marketing mix. Thus, different product formulations, different levels of promotional effort, and so on can be tested in the market place to gauge their different effects.

Sometimes market experimentation can take place in laboratory condi- tions, particularly in the case of advertising. Samples of the target audience will be exposed to the advertisement and their reactions obtained. Eye cameras, polygraphs and tachistoscopes are just some of the devices that can be used to record physical reactions to marketing stimuli.

In contrast with such methods are those that are classified as *non-reactive* in that they do not rely on data derived directly from the respondent. Best known amongst these are *retail audits* and *consumer panels*, both widely used by consumer companies. Retail audits involve the regular monitoring of a representative sample of stockists. At regular periods the researcher visits the stockists and records the current level of stocks of the product group being audited and the delivery notes for any such goods delivered since his last visit. With the information on stock levels on his last visit, it is now a simple matter to determine sales of the audited items, i.e. opening stock + deliveries between visits − closing stock = sales during the period.

The consumer panel is simply a sample group of consumers who record in a diary their purchases and consumption over a period of time. This technique has been used in industrial as well as consumer markets and can provide continuous data on usage patterns as well as much other useful data.

Finally, and in many respects, the most important of all marketing research methods is the use of existing materials, particularly by means of *desk research*, which should always be the starting point of any marketing research programme. There is often a wealth of information to be obtained from published information such as government statistics, OECD, EEC, the United Nations, newspapers, technical journals, trade association publications, published market surveys, and so on. Two or three days spent on desk research nearly always provides pleasant surprises for the company that believes it lacks information about its markets. When combined with internal sales information, this can be the most powerful research method open to a company.

Marketing intelligence systems

Given the importance of information to marketing decision-making, it is clear that time spent on the proper organization of information flows will be a sound investment. Such organization is often referred to as the *marketing intelligence system* (MIS). Much research has been carried out in this area to show that it is one of the most badly organized areas of management, in spite of the advent of the computer. This has been shown to be largely a function of the failure of management to identify the decisions that have to be taken and the information essential to making these decisions.

Clearly the definition of management information needs is central to the successful construction of a MIS, but it is this vital step which is rarely completed properly. This is mostly because executives fail to isolate the key determinants of success. For example, they misunderstand the meaning and significance of market share, or they over- or under-estimate the importance of service levels, and so on. The result is inevitably the kind of 'snow job' that is so evident in many companies in which data and information are produced on a regular basis in such volumes that it becomes virtually impossible for the recipients to isolate what is or is not important. Consequently the output of such a system is rarely used and management continues to operate largely on the basis of intuition and hunch. The model shown in Figure 11.1 is a helpful guide to the construction of a MIS.

There are four steps that are essential for the successful construction of a MIS. Firstly, make a detailed list of all current data and information that are produced.

Secondly, get each manager to list the decisions he has to make, together with the information essential to the making of these decisions.

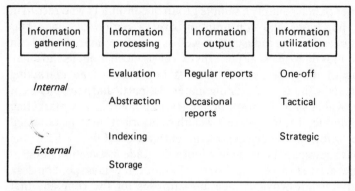

Information gathering	Information processing	Information output	Information utilization
	Evaluation	Regular reports	One-off
Internal			
	Abstraction	Occasional reports	Tactical
	Indexing		Strategic
External			
	Storage		

Figure 11.1

Thirdly, combine these two in the most logical manner, since there will be many redundancies in information requirements. Taking as an example internally generated sales data, it should be possible to make a list of all possible combinations of the following: product lines; product line summaries; trade categories; geographical areas; time scales; comparatives; purchasing patterns; etc.

All of these can be combined, in code form, on a matrix. Now comes the most difficult part of all. Looking at every one of the many combinations, write down the purpose for which each of the reports is required. For example, in respect of a regularly produced product line report, its basic purpose would be to provide definitive performance information on simple product lines within defined geographical areas. Thus, the objectives of a monthly report listing product lines sales by trade category might be:

1 To identify the proportionate spread and penetration of individual product lines by trade category. This is important if the company is seeking to establish brands in specific market sectors as a means of market segmentation.
2 To assess outlet penetration of new products.
3 To assess loss of sales in outlets.
4 To facilitate customer and outlet targeting.
5 To facilitate evaluation of outlet promotional activity.
6 To facilitate comparison of actual sales to potential; and so on.

Finally, there is the difficult task of organizing the system. Having worked out the 'ideal' MIS, it is now necessary to evaluate its cost, for clearly while it is tempting to think in terms of building a totally integrated MIS from first principles, experience suggests that it is better to think 'total' but to plan 'piecemeal'.

Adopting a building block approach, each block of which represents a sub-system for meeting a discrete information need, will eventually enable a totally integrated and sophisticated system to be developed in accordance with the needs and experience of the users. However, while the benefits of collecting and storing disaggregated data are obvious, the problem is that maintaining disaggregated files is expensive and management must balance this extra cost against the possibility that future market developments may require system modifications which cannot be made because data has been aggregated.

Organizational aspects of MIS

Because the MIS is part of a company-wide information system, it could be argued that it should be located within a central corporate information office so that the integration which is so desirable within the marketing function also takes place on a company-wide basis. However, the main issue is not so much where in an organization the information function should be located, as how best, given the constraints of the existing marketing organizational set-up (which will be a function of needs largely dictated by the market place), to facilitate both vertical and horizontal information flows both into and out of the information unit. Thus, while either a central company intelligence unit or a marketing department based unit would suffice, the problem is really that of institutionalizing procedures, through systems, to facilitate information flows, and training management in their use. The inputs would come from all levels of management through systematized procedures, as either items of information or requests for information. The information unit would sift and check the information, analyse it, decide where within the organization it might be useful and transmit the information to potential users or store it for future use.

Thus, the MIS may be managed by a group within the marketing department, or as part of an overall company system.

Forecasting

Forecasting is one of the most emotive subjects in the whole field of management. Most managers reckon to be experts, or at least are rarely backward in expressing an opinion about the subject, and the marketing man is constantly on the rack, because the one task he inevitably gets wrong is the forecast.

While in a book of this kind it is not possible to go into any detail, it would be wrong not to attempt to put this subject into a better perspective than it is currently.

Why is forecasting so difficult?

The size and complexity of the marketing task in all kinds of enterprise have substantially increased in recent years.

The growing diversity of customer needs in a rapidly-changing environment has resulted in shorter product life cycles, which have therefore become more difficult to manage profitably. Distribution patterns have changed dramatically in most markets, and competitive pressures have intensified with the geographic dispersion of operations and the growing internationalization of the scale of businesses, the management of which has become more competent as a result of the growing professionalism of management educators. The socio-cultural, legal, political environments in which managers have to operate have become more volatile and subject to more rapid change. The volume of data and information available has mushroomed, and processing networks have become more sophisticated, while the availability of quantitative techniques to the management of the marketing function has outpaced the ability to use them effectively. Added to this is the ever-present difficulty of measuring the behavioural aspects of marketing, such as social, cultural and psychological.

The result of all this is that it is becoming increasingly more difficult to find and develop profitable markets, and with this comes the difficulty of forecasting with anything like the accuracy that was possible when markets were more stable. Nevertheless, it has to be done and it has to be done well, because the consequences of being wrong can be very severe indeed for a company.

This is not the place to go into a detailed description of the many forecasting techniques available to a company. However, it could be useful to discuss briefly the major boundaries of forecasting as outlined in Figure 11.2.

From this it will be seen that there are two major types of forecasting which can be loosely described as *macro* and *micro*. Selection of the appropriate technique is dependent on four main factors, the first of which is

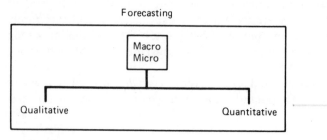

Figure 11.2

the degree of accuracy required. It will be obvious that the greater the risk of the decision that depends on the forecast, the greater will be the accuracy required, hence the cost. Secondly, the method will depend on the availability of data and information. Thirdly, the time horizon is a key determinant of the forecasting method. For example, are we forecasting next period's sales, in which case quantitative extrapolative approaches may be appropriate, or are we forecasting what will happen to our principal market over the next five years, in which case qualitative approaches may be appropriate? Lastly, the position of the product in its life cycle will also be a key determinant of the forecasting method. For example, at the introductory stage of a product's life cycle, less data and information will be available than at the maturity stage, when time series can be a useful forecasting method.

From this it will be apparent immediately that we must make an important distinction between macro and micro forecasting. Macro forecasting is essentially concerned with forecasting markets in total, whereas micro forecasting is more concerned with detailed unit forecasts. The discussion in Chapter 2 of the marketing planning process makes it very clear that budgets and plans which are based on little more than trend extrapolations are unlikely to be successful in the long run, since the really key strategic issues relating to products and markets are rarely given due consideration through such a process. Likewise, it will be recalled that in Chapter 4 in our discussion of market segmentation, it was stressed that there are inherent dangers in running sophisticated budgeting systems that are based on little more than crude extrapolations of past sales trends and which leave the marketing strategies implicit. Such systems are the ones that cause serious commercial problems when market structures change.

Thus, some form of macro forecasting has to precede the setting of marketing objectives and strategies, while detailed unit forecasts, or micro forecasts, should come after the company has decided which specific market opportunities it wants to take advantage of and how best this can be done.

Figure 11.2 also shows that there are basically two major techniques for forecasting which can be described as *qualitative* and *quantitative*. It would be unusual if either of these methods was used entirely on its own, mainly because of the inherent dangers in each. What we are really talking about is the need to combine an intuitive approach with the purely mathematical approach.

For example, it is comparatively easy to develop an equation which will extrapolate statistically the world population up to, say, the year 2000. The problem with such an approach, however, is that it does not take account of likely changes in past trends. It would be easy to list a whole series of possible events which could affect world population, and then assign probabilities to the likelihood of those events happening.

The main point we are making is that it is the task of management to take whatever relevant data are available to help predict the future, to use on them whatever quantitative techniques are appropriate, but then to use qualitative methods such as expert opinions, market research, analogy, and so on to predict what will be the likely *discontinuities* in the time series. It is only through the sensible use of the available tools that management will begin to understand what has to be done to match its own capabilities with carefully selected market needs. Without such an understanding, any form of forecasting is likely to be a sterile exercise.

Organizing for marketing planning

The purpose of this brief section is not to delve into the complexities of organizational forms, but to put the difficult process of marketing planning into the context of the relevant environment in which it will be taking place. The point is that you start from where you *are*, not from where you would like to be, and it is a fact of business that marketing means different things in different circumstances. It is not our intention here to recommend any one particular organizational form. Rather it is to point out some of the more obvious organizational issues and their likely effect on the way marketing planning is carried out.

Firstly, as firms grow in sales, so they tend to go through an organizational evolution. Figure 11.3 shows a firm starting off its existence and growing in turnover over a period of time. When such a firm starts off, it is often organized totally around the owner who tends to know more about his customers and products than anyone else in the company. This organizational form can be represented as in Figure 11.4, with all decisions and lines of communication revolving around one person. The point here is that formal-

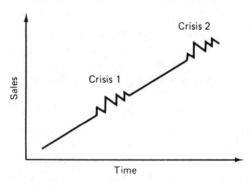

Figure 11.3

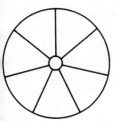

Figure 11.4

ized marketing planning by means of systems and written procedures is probably less relevant than in, say, a diversified multinational.

However, as this firm grows in size and complexity, as new products and new markets are added, this organizational form begins to break down and the first crisis appears, which is resolved in one of two ways. Either the owner/entrepreneur sells his business and retires or starts up again, or he adopts the more traditional organizational form with which most of us are familiar (Figure 11.5) in which certain functional duties are allocated to individuals to manage by means of their own specialized departments.

This often solves the immediate problem, but sometimes the firm grows so big and diverse that a second crisis occurs, typically caused when the decisions of one functional department begin to have an adverse effect on another functional department.

Our research at Cranfield shows that in high-growth markets, even when such crises occur, firms muddle through and survive and prosper, but often at the expense of lost profit, management frustration, and the like. In stagnant or low-growth markets, firms come to realize that the word 'synergy' is not just a theoretical concept and begin to strive towards taking a more cohesive approach to their markets. It is here that often the first *serious* attempts are made at formalized marketing planning.

Within this second phase of growth, there are basically two kinds of organization which can be described as either *decentralized* or *centralized*, with several combinations within each extreme.

Looking firstly at decentralization, it is possible to represent this diagram-

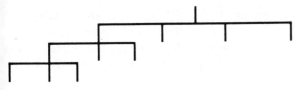

Figure 11.5

matically as in Figure 11.6.* The shaded area of the triangle represents the top level strategic management of the firm. It can be seen from this diagram that the central services, such as market research and public relations are repeated at the subsidiary company level. It can also be seen that there is a strategic level of management at the subsidiary level, the acid test being whether subsidiary company/unit top management can introduce new products without reference to headquarters.

The point about this kind of decentralized organizational structure is that it leads inevitably to duplication of effort and differentiation of strategies, with all the consequent problems, unless a major effort is made to get some synergy out of the several systems by means of a company-wide planning system. One telecommunications company had a range of 1500 products and one of those products had 1300 different variations, all of which was the result of a totally decentralized marketing-orientated approach in the subsidiary companies. It was not surprising that any sensible economies of scale in production were virtually impossible, with the result that the company made a substantial loss. The same problems apply to marketing research, advertising, pricing, distribution, and other business areas. When someone takes the trouble to find out, it is often very salutary to see the reaction of senior managers at headquarters when they are told, for example, that the very same market problem is being researched in many different countries around the world, all at enormous expense.

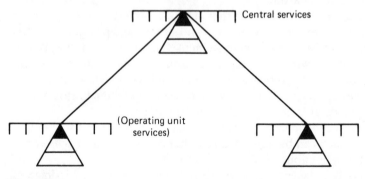

Figure 11.6

It is this kind of organization structure which, above all others, requires strong central coordination by means of some kind of planning system, otherwise everyone wastes enormous amounts of corporate resources striving to maximize their own small part of the business. If, however, some

---

*This section owes much to the original work and thinking of Simon Majaro.

system can be found of gaining synergy from all the energy expended, then the rewards are great indeed. The point is, that marketing in this kind of system means something different from marketing in other kinds of system, and it is as well to recognize this from the outset.

A centrally controlled company tends to look as depicted in Figure 11.7. Here it will be seen that there is no *strategic* level of management in the subsidiary units, particularly in respect of new product introductions. This kind of organizational form tends to lead to standardized strategies, particularly in respect of product management. For example, when a new product is introduced, it tends to be designed at the outset with as many markets as possible in mind, while the benefits from market research in one area are passed on to other areas, and so on. The problem here, of course, is that unless great care is exercised, subsidiary units can easily become less sensitive to the needs of individual markets, and hence lose flexibility in reacting to competitive moves. The point here again, is that marketing in this kind of system means something different from marketing in the kind of system described above.

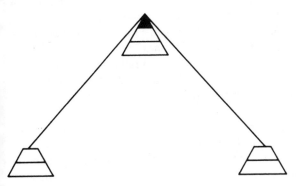

Figure 11.7

There is a difference between financial manipulation and business management in respect of the headquarters role. There is a difference between a corporation and its individual components, and often there is confusion about what kind of planning should be done by managers at varying levels in the organization, such confusion arising because the chief executive has not made it clear what kind of business he is managing.

We have looked briefly at two principal organizational forms, both of which consist essentially of a central office and various decentralized divisions, each with its own unique products, processes and markets which complement the others in the group. In enterprises of this type, planning within the divisions applies to the exploration of markets and improved efficiency within the boundaries laid down by headquarters. The problems and opportunities that this method throws up tends to make the head-quarters role one of classifying the boundaries for the enterprise as a whole, in relation to new products and markets that do not appear to fall within the scope of one of the divisions.

In this type of organization, the managers of affiliated companies are normally required to produce the level of profit set by headquarters management within the constraints imposed on them and such companies need to institutionalize this process by providing a formal structure of ideas and systems so that operating management know what they are expected to do and whether they are doing the essential things. The point about these kinds of organization seems to be that some method *has* to be found of planning and controlling the growth of the business in order to utilize effectively the evolving skills and growing reputation of the firm, and so avoid an uncontrolled dissipation of energy. It is probably easier to do this in a centrally organized firm, but as we have pointed out, both organizational forms have their disadvantages.

Finally, the *financial trust* type of organization needs to be mentioned briefly, in which the primary concern of central management is the investment of shareholders' capital in various businesses. The buying and selling of interests in various firms is done for appreciation of capital rather than for building an enterprise with any logic of its own. Planning in this type of operation requires different knowledge and skills, and addresses itself to kinds of problems that are different from those in the two organizational forms described above.

Before going on to describe marketing planning systems, there are two further points worth making briefly about organizing for marketing. The first is that where marketing and sales are separated at board level, marketing planning is going to be a very different kind of activity from a situation in which both functions are coordinated at board level. Figure 11.8 illustrates these two different situations.

In the first of these organizational forms, marketing is very much a staff activity, with the real power vested in the sales organization. While a strong chief executive can ensure that the two activities are sensibly coordinated, unfortunately this rarely happens effectively because he is often too busy with production, distribution, personnel, and financial issues to devote enough of his time to sales and marketing. The point here is that a sales force is quite correctly concerned with *today's* products, problems, customers, and so on, while a marketing manager needs to be thinking about the *future*. The sales force is also quite correctly concerned mainly with *individual* products, problems and customers, while a marketing manager needs to be thinking about *groups* of products and customers (portfolio management

(a)

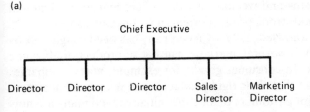

(b)

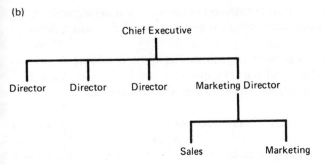

Figure 11.8

and market segmentation). The two jobs are closely connected, but fundamentally different, and great care is necessary to ensure that what the marketing department is *planning* is the same as what the sales force is actually *doing* in the field. All too often they are not.

The second kind of organizational form tends to make it easier to ensure a sensible coordination between planning and doing.

The second and final part about marketing organizational forms is that there are a number of issues that *all* firms have to address. These are:

Functions (such as advertising, market research, pricing, and so on)
Products
Markets
Geographical locations
Channels

Of these, most firms would readily agree that in most cases the two main issues are *products* and *markets*, which is why many companies have what are called 'product managers' and/or 'market managers'. There can be no right or wrong answer to the question of which of these is the better, and commonsense will dictate that it is market circumstances alone that will determine which is most appropriate for any one company.

Each has its strengths and weaknesses. A product manager orientated system will ensure good strong product orientation, but can also easily lead to superficial market knowledge. Many a company has been caught out by subtle changes in their several markets causing a product to become practically redundant. In consumer goods, for example, many companies are beginning to admit that their rigid product/brand management system has allowed their major customers to take the initiative, and many are now changing belatedly to a system where the focus of marketing activity revolves around major customer/market groups rather than individual products.

On the other hand, a market manager orientated system can easily result in unnecessary product differentiation and poor *overall* product development.

Ideally, therefore, whatever organizational form is adopted, the two central issues of products and markets constantly need to be addressed. This conundrum can be summarized in the following brief case study.

Northern Sealants Limited manufactures a range of adhesives that fall into two main categories: seals; and sealants. The company supplies these products to a large number of markets. However, the main users come under four industry headings: gas, oil and petrochemical refineries; automotive; electrical; and OEM. Advise how the marketing function should be organized.

Figure 11.9 illustrates this case diagrammatically in what is often referred to as a *matrix* organization. Figure 11.10 puts this structure into the context of this particular company. Here it will be seen that organizationally

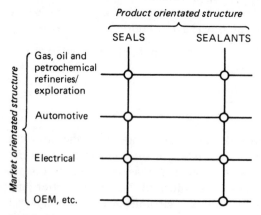

Figure 11.9

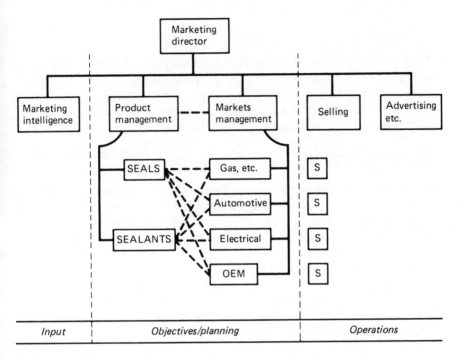

Figure 11.10

Northern Sealants have both a product management and market management structure. The basic role of the product manager is to ensure that the
aspects of the product are properly managed, while the role of the market
manager is to pay particular attention to the needs of the market. Close
liaison between the two is obviously necessary and a basic principle of this
kind of organization is that ultimate authority for the final decision *must* be
vested in either one or the other. Even when this is done, however,
communications can still be difficult, and great care is necessary to ensure
that vested interests are not allowed to dominate the real product/market
issues.

To summarize, no one particular organizational form can be recommended, commonsense and market needs being the final arbiters. However,
the following factors *always* need to be considered:

Marketing 'centres of gravity'
Interface areas (e.g. present/future; salesmen/drawing office; etc.)
Authority and responsibility

Ease of communication
Coordination
Flexibility
Human factors

What is certain is that one of the major determinants of the effectiveness of any marketing planning which is attempted within a company will be the way that it organizes for marketing. The purpose of this section has been to point out some of the more obvious facts and pitfalls before attempting to outline a marketing planning system, to which we can now turn.

Application questions

1   Over what period of time do you forecast in your organization? Is it the right period? Do all relevant managers have an opportunity to make a contribution? If not, say how they could become involved.
2   Is there ever a significant variance between forecasts and sales? If so, how do you explain it?
3   What additional information would you like to help you make more accurate forecasts? How could you obtain such information? Why have you not obtained it in the past?
4   Describe any piece of marketing research that in your view has had a major impact on your company's operations.
5   Describe any major decisions taken which in your view required market research before they were made.
6   Describe what your company's major problems are in the way it uses marketing research.
7   If you were to establish a new marketing information system for your company, say what it would contain. Where is it different from your current one and how could such a system be organized and made to work?

12 Designing and Implementing a Marketing Planning System

In Chapter 3 we explained some of the many myths that surround marketing planning and spelt out the conditions that must be satisfied if any company is to have an effective marketing planning system. These are:

1 Any closed-loop marketing planning system (but especially one that is essentially a forecasting and budgeting system) will lead to entropy of marketing and creativity. Therefore, there has to be some mechanism for preventing inertia from setting in through the over-bureaucratization of the system.

2 Marketing planning undertaken at the functional level of marketing, in the absence of a means of integration with other functional areas of the business at general management level, will be largely ineffective.

3 The separation of responsibility for operational and strategic marketing planning will lead to a divergence of the short-term thrust of a business at the operational level from the long-term objectives of the enterprise as a whole. This will encourage a preoccupation with short-term results at operational level, which normally makes the firm less effective in the long term.

4 Unless the chief executive understands and takes an active role in marketing planning, it will never be an effective system.

5 A period of up to three years is necessary (especially in large firms) for the successful introduction of an effective marketing planning system.

Some indication of the potential complexity of marketing planning can be seen in Figure 12.1. Even in a generalized model such as this, it can be seen that in a large diversified group operating in many foreign markets, a complex combination of product, market and functional plans is possible. For example, what is required at regional level will be different from what is

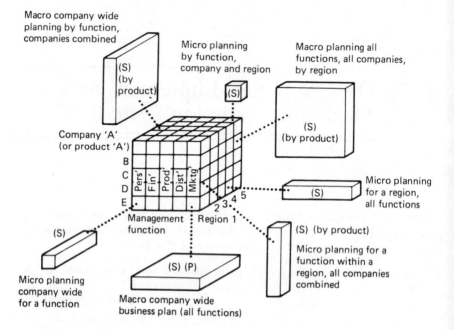

Macro business plan, all functions, all companies, all regions
together with constituent building blocks

Macro company wide
planning by function,
companies combined

Micro planning
by function,
company and region

Macro planning all
functions, all companies,
by region

(S)
(by
product)

(S)

(S)
(by product)

Company 'A'
(or product 'A')

B
C
D   Pers' Fin' Prod' Dist' Mktg'
E

Micro planning
for a region,
all functions

(S)

2 3 4 5

Management   Region 1
function

(S) (by product)

(S)

Micro planning for a
function within a
region, all companies
combined

(S) (P)

Micro planning
company wide
for a function

Macro company wide
business plan (all functions)

Key P = parent company
    S = subsidiary company

Figure 12.1

required at headquarters level, while it is clear that the total corporate plan has to be built from the individual building blocks. Furthermore, the function of marketing itself may be further functionalized for the purpose of planning, such as marketing research, advertising, selling, distribution, promotion, and so forth, while different customer groups may need to have separate plans drawn up.

Let us be dogmatic about requisite planning levels. Firstly, in a large diversified group, irrespective of such organizational issues, anything other than a systematic approach approximating to a formalized marketing planning system is unlikely to enable the necessary control to be exercised over the corporate identity.

Secondly, unnecessary planning, or overplanning, could easily result from an inadequate or indiscriminate consideration of the real planning needs at the different levels in the hierarchical chain.

Thirdly, as size and diversity grow, so the degree of formalization of the marketing planning process must also increase. This can be simplified in the form of a matrix (Figure 12.2).

The degree of formalization must increase with the evolving size and diversity of operations. However, while the degree of formalization will change, the need for a complete marketing planning system does not. The problems that companies suffer, then, are a function of either the degree to which they have a requisite marketing planning system or the degree to which the formalization of their system grows with the situational complexities attendant upon the size and diversity of operations.

It has already been stressed that central to the success of any enterprise is the objective-setting process. Connected with this is the question of the design of the planning system, and in particular, the question of who should be involved in what, and how. For example, who should carry out the situation review, state the assumptions, set marketing objectives, and strategies, and carry out the scheduling and costing-out programme, and at what level?

These complex issues revolve essentially around two dimensions—the size of the company, and the degree of business diversity. There are, of course, many other issues, such as whether a company is operating through subsidiary companies or through agents, but these can only be considered against the background of the two major dimensions of size and diversity.

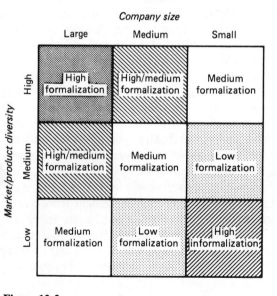

Figure 12.2

Size

Of these two dimensions, size of operations is without doubt the biggest determinant of the type of marketing planning system used.

In small companies, there is rarely much diversity of products or markets, and top management has an in-depth knowledge of the key determinants of success and failure. There is usually a high level of knowledge of both the technology and the market. While in such companies the central control mechanism is the sales forecast and budget, top managers are able to explain the rationale lying behind the numbers, have a very clear view of their comparative strengths and weaknesses, and are able to explain the company's marketing strategy without difficulty. This understanding and familiarity with the strategy is shared with key operating subordinates by means of personal, face-to-face dialogue throughout the year. Subordinates are operating within a logical framework of ideas, which they understand. There is a shared understanding between top and middle management of the industry and prevailing business conditions. In such cases, since either the owner or a director is usually also deeply involved in the day-to-day management of the business, the need to rely on informational inputs from subordinates is considerably less than in larger companies. Consequently, there is less need for written procedures about marketing audits, SWOT analyses, assumptions, and marketing objectives and strategies, as these are carried out by top management, often informally at meetings and in face-to-face discussions with subordinates, the results of which are the basis of the forecasts and budgets. Written documents in respect of price, advertising, selling, and so on, are very brief, but those managers responsible for those aspects of the business know what part they are expected to play in achieving the company's objectives. Such companies are, therefore, operating according to a set of structured procedures, and complete the several steps in the marketing planning process, but in a relatively informal manner.

On the other hand, many small companies that have a poor understanding of the marketing concept and in which the top manager leaves his strategy implicit, suffer many serious operational problems.

These operational problems become progressively worse as the size of company increases. As the number and level of management increase, it becomes progressively more difficult for top management to enjoy an in-depth knowledge of industry and business conditions by informal, face-to-face means. In the absence of written procedures and a structured framework, the different levels of operating management become increasingly less able to react in a rational way to day-to-day pressures. Systems of tight budgeting control, without the procedures outlined in this book, are in the main only successful in situations of buoyant trading conditions, are often the cause of high levels of management frustration, and are seen to be a major contributory factor in those cases where eventual decline sets in.

In general, the bigger the company, the greater is the incidence of standardized, formalized procedures for the several steps in the marketing planning process.

Diversity of operations

From the point of view of management control, the least complex environment in which to work is an undiversified company. For the purpose of this discussion, 'undiversified' is taken to mean companies with limited product lines or homogeneous customer groups. For example, hydraulic hose could be sold to many diverse markets, or a diverse range of products could be sold into only one market such as say, the motor industry. Both could be classified as 'undiversified'.

In such cases, the need for institutionalized marketing planning systems increases with the size of the operation, and there is a strong relationship between size and the complexity of the management task, irrespective of any apparent diversity. For example, an oil company will operate in many diverse markets around the world, through many different kinds of marketing systems, and with varying levels of market growth and market share. In most respects, therefore, the control function for headquarters management is just as difficult and complex as that in a major, diversified conglomerate. The major difference is the greater level of in-depth knowledge which top management has about the key determinants of success and failure underlying the product or market worldwide, because of its homogeneity.

Because of this homogeneity of product or market, it is usually possible for headquarters to impose worldwide policies on operating units in respect of things such as certain aspects of advertising, public relations, packaging, pricing, trade marks, product development, and so on, whereas in the headquarters of a diversified conglomerate, overall policies of this kind tend to be impracticable and meaningless.

The view is often expressed that common planning in companies comprising many heterogeneous units is less helpful and confuses rather than improves understanding between operating units and headquarters. However, the truth is that conglomerates often consist of several smaller multinationals, some diversified, and some not, and that the actual task of marketing rests on the lowest level in an organization at which there is general management profit responsibility. Forecasting and budgeting systems by themselves rarely encourage anything but a short-term, parochial view of the business at these levels, and in the absence of the kind of marketing planning procedures described in this book, higher levels of management do not have a sufficiently rational basis on which to set long-term marketing objectives.

Exactly the same principles apply at the several levels of control in a diversified multinational conglomerate, in that at the highest level of control there has to be some rational basis on which to make decisions about the portfolio of investments, and in the Cranfield research, the most successful companies were those with standardized marketing planning procedures to aid this process. In such companies, there is a hierarchy of audits, SWOT analyses, assumptions, strategies and programmes, with increasingly more detail required in the procedures at the lowest levels in the organization. The precise details of each step vary according to circumstances, but the eventual output of the process is in a universally consistent form.

The basis on which the whole system rests is the informational input requirements at the highest level of command. Marketing objectives and strategies are frequently synthesized into a multidisciplinary corporate plan at the next general management profit-responsible level, until at the highest level of command the corporate plan consists largely of financial information and summaries of the major operational activities. This is an important point, for there is rarely a consolidated operational marketing plan at conglomerate headquarters. This often exists only at the lowest level of general management profit responsibility, and even here it is sometimes incorporated into the corporate plan, particularly in capital goods companies, where engineering, manufacturing and technical services are major factors in commercial success.

Here it is necessary to distinguish between short-term operational plans and long-term strategic plans, both products of the same process. Conglomerate headquarters are particularly interested in the progress of, and prospects for, the major areas of operational activities, and while obviously concerned to ensure a satisfactory current level of profitability, are less interested in the detailed short-term scheduling and costing-out of the activities necessary to achieve these objectives. This, however, is a major concern at the lowest level of general management profit responsibility.

To summarize, the smaller the company, the more informal and personal the procedures for marketing planning. As company size and diversity increases, so the need for institutionalized procedures increases.

The really important issue in any system is the degree to which it enables *control* to be exercised over the key determinants of success and failure. To a large extent, the issue, much debated in the literature, of where in an international organization responsibility for setting marketing objectives and strategies should lie, is something of a red herring. Of course, in a diversified multinational conglomerate, detailed marketing objectives and strategies for some remote country cannot be set by someone in London. It is precisely this issue, i.e. finding the right balance between the flexibility of operating units to react to changes in local market conditions and centralized control, that a formally designed system seeks to tackle. Those companies which conform to the framework outlined here have systems which, through a hierarchy of bottom up/top down negotiating procedures, reach a nice balance between the need for detailed control at the lowest level of operations and centralized control. The main role of headquarters is to harness the company's strengths on a worldwide basis and to ensure that lower level decisions do not cause problems in other areas and lead to wasteful duplication.

Figure 12.3 explores four key outcomes that marketing planning can evoke. It can be seen that systems I, III and IV, i.e. where the individual is totally subordinate to a formalized system, or where individuals are allowed to do what they want without any system, or where there is neither system

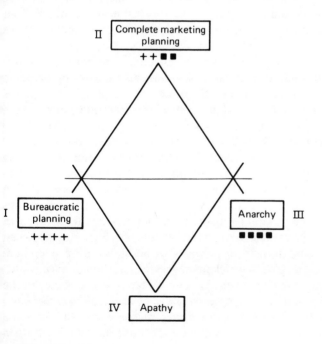

+ Degree of formalization
■ Degree of openness

Figure 12.3

nor creativity, are less successful than system II, in which the individual is allowed to be entrepreneurial within a total system. System II, then, will be an effective marketing planning system, but one in which the degree of formalization will be a function of company size and diversity.

Creativity cannot flourish in a closed-loop formalized system. There would be little disagreement that in today's abrasive, turbulent, and highly competitive environment, it is those firms that succeed in extracting entrepreneurial ideas and creative marketing programmes from systems that are necessarily yet acceptably formalized, that will succeed in the long run. Much innovative flair can so easily get stifled by systems.

Certainly there is ample evidence of international companies with highly formalized systems that produce stale and repetitive plans, with little changed from year to year and that fail to point up the really key strategic issues as a result. The scandalous waste this implies is largely due to a *lack of personal intervention by key managers during the early stages of the planning cycle.*

There is clearly a need, therefore, to find a way of perpetually renewing the planning life cycle each time around. Inertia must never set in. Without some such valve or means of opening up the loop, inertia quickly produces decay.

Such a valve has to be inserted early in the planning cycle during the audit, or situation review stage. In companies with effective marketing planning systems, whether such systems are formalized or informal, the critical intervention of senior managers, from the chief executive down through the hierarchical chain, comes at the audit stage. Essentially what takes place is a personalized presentation of audit findings, together with proposed marketing objectives and strategies and outline budgets for the strategic planning period. These are discussed, amended where necessary, and agreed in various synthesized formats at the hierarchical levels in the organization *before* any detailed operational planning takes place. It is at such meetings that managers are called upon to justify their views, which tends to force them to be more bold and creative than they would have been had they been allowed merely to send in their proposals. Obviously, however, even here much depends on the degree to which managers take a critical stance, which is much greater when the chief executive himself takes an active part in the process. *Every hour of time devoted at this stage by the chief executive has a multiplier effect throughout the remainder of the process.* And let it be remembered we are not, repeat not, talking about budgets at this juncture in anything other than outline form.

Until recently it was believed that there may well be fundamental differences in marketing planning approaches, depending on factors such as the type of industrial goods and markets involved, company size, the degree of dependence on overseas sales, and the methods used to market goods abroad. In particular, the much debated role of headquarters management in the marketing planning process is frequently put forward as being a potential cause of great difficulty.

One of the most encouraging findings to emerge from the Cranfield research is that the theory of marketing planning is universally applicable, and that such issues are largely irrelevant. While the planning task is less complicated in small, undiversified companies, and there is less need for formalized procedures than in large, diversified companies, the fact is that exactly the same framework should be used in all circumstances, and that this approach brings similar benefits to all.

In a multinational conglomerate, headquarters management is able to assess major trends in products and markets around the world, and is thus able to develop strategies for investment, expansion, diversification and divestment on a global basis. For their part, subsidiary management can develop appropriate strategies with a sense of locomotion towards the achievement of coherent overall goals.

This is achieved by means of synthesized information flows from the bottom upwards, which facilitates useful comparison of performance around the world, and the diffusion of valuable information, skills, experiences and systems from the top downwards. The particular benefits which accrue to companies using such systems can be classified under the major headings of the marketing mix elements as follows:

Marketing information There is a transfer of knowledge, a sharing of expertise and an optimization of effort around the world.
Product Control is exercised over the product range. Maximum effectiveness is gained by concentrating on certain products in certain markets, based on experience gained throughout the world.
Price Pricing policies are sufficiently flexible to enable local management to trade effectively, while the damaging effects of interaction are considerably mitigated.
Place Substantial gains are made by rationalization of the logistics function.
Promotion Duplication of effort and a multitude of different platforms/company images are ameliorated. Efforts in one part of the world reinforce those in another.

The procedures which facilitate the provision of such information and knowledge transfers also encourage operational management to think strategically about their own areas of responsibility, instead of managing only for the short term.

It is abundantly clear that it is through a marketing planning system and planning skills that such benefits are achieved, and that discussions such as those about the standardization of marketing strategies in the absence of some form of standardized *process* are largely irrelevant. Any standardization that may be possible will become clear only if a company can successfully develop a system for identifying the needs of each market and each segment in which it operates, and for organizing resources to satisfy those needs in such a way that best resource utilization results worldwide.

The marketing planning process redefined: a summary

The purpose of this section is to summarize the earlier chapters, and to ensure that the many threads developed are seen in their correct context, within the marketing planning process.

There are many checklists of things you have to do to go through the motions of marketing planning. But pages of figures and marketing prose, well typed, elegantly bound, and retrievably filed, does not make much difference. It makes some, because the requirements of writing a plan demand deep thought. However, it is vital that companies must always search for the *requisite level of marketing planning*, just as in engineering you will often seek the requisite level of variety in product or services offered.

It is well to remember, above all else, what the *purpose* of marketing planning is. The following sub-sections are intended to summarize the main points of a requisite marketing planning system, and to provide the basis for the design of a system suitable for any business.

The process itself

'How well should we be doing in present trading conditions?' The answer to this question requires considerable analysis inside and outside the company. Simply looking at the bottom line and saying 'budget achieved' is not enough. It is quite possible to achieve budget and still lose market share—if the budget is not developed from a proper qualitative assessment of the market *in the first place*.

The real question we should be asking is *'What sales/gross profits should we be achieving in the current trading conditions?'* To answer the above questions, it is necessary to have available a well argued 'common format' in the organization, i.e. a marketing plan.

Undertaking marketing planning is like 'trying to nail a jelly to the wall'; it is a messy process which evolves over time. In effect you are attempting to 'control' the future by deciding *what to do about the possible different trading environments*. In undertaking marketing planning you join the ranks of those who 'make things happen' in the company. The alternative is to be tossed around like a cork in the sea of competition.

The marketing planning process involves the bringing together of minds within the company/group/department, and a 'trading off' between the difficult issues raised. By definition, the marketing planning process starts from a 'zero base' each year; the 10 per cent syndrome must be avoided at all times.

The marketing planning process facilitates, and indeed depends on, interactive communication up and down the organization. If this does not happen, all that results are forecasts projected from history rather than the development of genuine objectives based on what is actually happening inside and outside the company.

Remember, the planning process is first and foremost to help you help yourself; it is not something you take part in simply to appease your superiors.

It is sometimes difficult for higher echelons in the organization to synthesize and aggregate the SWOTs from lower levels. However, the task is made easier if, for instance, departments are grouped to reflect the structure of the external market.

Once the marketing planning process has developed through to the budget stage, and this budget is agreed, then commitment must be total. If however, during the course of the ensuing fiscal year, performance begins to fall behind budget, it is quite legitimate to manipulate any and all elements of the marketing plan in order to collect the deficit. So there is flexibility in the way the elements of a plan can be altered and manipulated; the budget however remains fixed.

Marketing audit

The marketing planning process starts with an *audit* of the company's operating performance and environment. The marketing audit is essentially a *data base* of all market-related issues with which the company is concerned. The subsequent SWOT analysis lends structure to the audit in order to facilitate on-going planning activities.

The company must provide a list of detailed questions which each manager is required to consider for his area of responsibility. Each manager carrying out his audit will use sales data and the company marketing information system to complete his audit. If the company has a marketing research manager, it is helpful at this stage if he can issue to all managers a market overview covering major market and product trends, etc.

It will probably be necessary to customize the audit checklist contents according to the level in the organization to which it is addressed. In this way, each particular checklist is made meaningful and relevant to each level. Some brief explanatory definitions may also be necessary.

The audit will inevitably require more data preparation than is finally reproduced in the marketing plan. Therefore, managers should attempt to start a 'product/market bible' during the year which can also be used as a reference source at verbal presentations of proposals, etc. What this means is that the marketing audit should be conducted on a *continuing* (dynamic) basis rather than at a particular point in time. In this way it becomes a useful information source to draw on for decision-making throughout the year.

Do not try to hide behind vague items in the audit, like 'poor economic condition'. Even in overall static or declining markets there will be 'growth' points present. Seek these out and decide whether or not to focus/concentrate your efforts on them.

Incorporate product life cycles and portfolio matrices as an integral part of the audit. The diagrams and the corresponding words should match.

The audit can be a useful 'transfer' device for when one manager moves job and another takes over. For example, the incoming manager can quickly pick up an understanding of that department's business.

SWOT analysis

It is important to remember that it is only the SWOT analysis, *not* the audit, that actually appears in the marketing plan. This summary of the audit should, if possible, contain not more than four or five pages of commentary focusing on *key* factors only. It should list internal *differential* strengths and weaknesses *vis à vis* competitors and key external opportunities and threats. A summary of reasons for good or bad performance should be included.

The SWOT analysis should be interesting to read, contain concise statements, include only the relevant and important data, and give greater emphasis to creative analysis.

It is suggested that the manager draws a product life cycle for each of his major products and uses the audit information to attempt to predict the future shape of the life cycle. It is also suggested that the manager plots his products on a portfolio matrix and that he uses the audit information to show the futute desired position of his products (e.g. for five years ahead, if this is the planning horizon. The matrix may, therefore, have to include some new products not currently in the range).

To be true marketers we must differentiate ourselves from our competitors. The SWOT analysis is a device which assists us to do that.

A SWOT analysis, well done, helps to identify and pin down the real issues which should be addressed in the future as a matter of priority. Too often however, the SWOT summary is just a smorgasbord of apparently unrelated points (in which case any underlying theme is difficult to discern).

Having listened to someone presenting a SWOT summary, you should end up with a clear understanding of the main thrust of their business. If a SWOT is well done, someone else should be able to draft the objectives which logically flow from it. The SWOT statement should contain clear indicators as to the key determinants of success in the company/group/department; we can then build on these.

The SWOT statement should, in effect, encapsulate our perception of the market place; summarize what we are trying to do; and point out required future actions. If pursued aggressively, this approach will make competitors, followers.

The SWOT is by definition a summary of the key issues emanating out of the marketing audit. The SWOT is generated from internal debate; it is not just one person's opinion. The SWOT should provide answers to such questions as:

What do customers need?
How do they buy?
What are our competitors doing?

Generally, the SWOT should be differential or at least the S and W (internal) part should be. The O and T (external) part of the SWOT is generally non-differential, e.g. the threat of a new sales tax. We have to assess the impact of such a threat (should it happen) earlier than our competitors, and make the appropriate preparations earlier in order to give us the edge.

In writing down an issue in our SWOT summary, we should continually follow with the implied question: 'Which means that . . .?' In this way we are forced to think about the implications of the issue itself.

Finally agreed budgets (which come at the end of the process) must reflect internal consistency with the issues raised in the original SWOT analysis. Often this internal consistency is not evident because budgets are done first rather than last, and the qualitative content is done last rather than first (in which case it is just rhetoric).

It is difficult to work to a SWOT prepared by another person, unless of course you were involved in the original debate. The quality of a SWOT analysis can suffer if:

1 Each item/issue is over-abbreviated.
2 If the writer concentrates on micro rather than macro issues.

Remember, it is a great self-discipline to complete a good tight but comprehensive SWOT.

Assumptions

These also should appear in the marketing plan. List the major assumptions on which the plan is based. If the plan can be implemented irrespective of any assumption made, then the assumption is unnecessary. They should be few in number and key.

Marketing objectives

These should also appear in the marketing plan. Marketing objectives are about products and markets only (*not* about advertising, etc.). The *words* used should reflect what appears in the product life cycle and in the portfolio matrix. Any figures used (such as volume, value, etc.) should also reflect this.

Note that if there is, say, a five-year planning horizon, the five-year marketing plan should contain overall marketing objectives with broad revenue and cost projections for the full five-year period. This plan will be required for the long-range corporate plan. The one-year marketing plan should contain the same overall marketing objectives plus the specific objectives for the first year of the planning cycle. Thereafter, the detailed one-year marketing plan should be about the next fiscal year only. Ideally, the one-year and five-year plans should be separate, but not necessarily so.

At an early stage in the planning process, it is likely that managers will have to discuss their major objectives with their superior prior to final agreement, since he will probably have a better understanding of the broader company objective.

It is necessary to set objectives in order to articulate to what we are in fact committing ourselves, and to force us to think about the corresponding resource implications.

Marketing objectives flow from the SWOT analysis and should be fully compatible with the key issues identified in the SWOT. Marketing objectives should be quantifiable and measurable for performance monitoring purposes; avoid directional terms such as 'improve', 'increase', 'expand', etc. There will be a hierarchy of marketing objectives down through the organization. Try to set priorities for your chosen marketing objectives.

Many so-called marketing objectives are in fact really marketing strategies—do not mix the two up. Marketing objectives are *what* we want to achieve; marketing strategies are *how* we intend to achieve the set objectives.

In some cases, marketing strategies and detailed marketing *actions* are confused. Actions are the short-term list of activities carried out to a schedule which in aggregate amount to a particular strategy.

Marketing strategies

These must also appear in the marketing plan. Strategies are how the objectives are to be achieved:

Product policies, to include functions, design, size, packaging, and so on.

Pricing policies to be followed for product groups in market segments.

Place policies for channels and customer service levels.

Promotion policies for communicating with customers under the relevant headings such as advertising, personal selling, sales promotion, etc.

Programmes

These must also appear in the marketing plan. Specific sub-objectives for products and segments supported by more detailed strategy and action statements, e.g. what, where, when, costs, etc. Here include *budgets* and *forecasts*, and of course a *consolidated budget*. The preparation of budgets and sales forecasts *must* reflect the marketing objectives. In turn the objectives, strategies and programmes *must* reflect the agreed budgets and sales forecasts.

Forecasts (in lieu of objectives) are obtained by simply extrapolating past experience. Instead, we should be taking a 'zero-based' view of the current and possible future environments in order to arrive at a viable set of objectives. Unit forecasts then follow.

The above noted zero-based review (in the form of a marketing audit and corresponding SWOT) is necessary in order to identify possible 'discontinuities' in our future trading environment; simple extrapolation of historical data ignores the possibility that discontinuities can (and do) occur.

Forecasts (and corresponding budgets based on such forecasts) can be self-fulfilling prophecies, e.g. salesmen sell the products they like to customers they enjoy selling to. If we project the resulting numbers by way of a forecast, we are *not* reflecting the real market situation.

A somewhat deeper perception of the market place is needed in order to review and reveal viable marketing objectives and strategies, which are consistent with the company's distinctive competence. Individual budget items must clearly be retraceable to issues identified in the original SWOT. When measuring performance, at all times seek to relate to the outside market as well as your internal budget.

Marketing plans

A written marketing plan (or plans) is the outcome of the marketing planning process. It is effectively a business proposition containing proposed courses of action which in turn have resource implications.

Written marketing plans verbalize (and formalize) our intuitive model of the market environment within which we operate. Written marketing plans help to make things happen.

The acid test of any marketing plan presentation is to ask yourself 'Would I put my own life's savings into the plan as presented?' If the answer is 'No', then further work is needed to refine your ideas.

A good discipline in preparing 'internally consistent' marketing plans is to use the following summary format:

SWOT
issues $\rightarrow$ Objective $\rightarrow$ Strategy $\rightarrow$ Specific actions and timing

Role of the chief executive in marketing planning

The Cranfield research showed that few chief executives have a clear perception of:

Purposes and methods of planning
Proper assignments of planning responsibilities throughout the organization
Proper structures and staffing of the planning department
Talent and skills required in an effective planning department

The role of the chief executive is generally agreed as being:

To define the organizational framework
To ensure the strategic analysis covers critical factors
To maintain the balance between short- and long-term results
To display his commitment to planning
To provide the entrepreneurial dynamic to overcome bureaucracy
To build this dynamic into the planning operation (motivation)

In respect of planning, his principal role is to open up the planning loop by means of his personal intervention. The main purpose of this is to act as a catalyst for the entrepreneurial dynamic within his organization, which can so easily decay through bureaucratization. This is not sufficiently recognized in the literature.

When considering this in the context of the reasons for failures of marketing planning systems, it is clear that, for any system to be effective, the chief executive requires to be conversant with planning techniques and approaches, and to be commited to and take part in the marketing planning process.

Role of the Planning Department in marketing planning

This raises the important question of the role of the planning department, which is:

To provide the planning structure and systems
To secure rapid data transmission in the form of intelligence
To act as a catalyst in obtaining inputs from operating divisions
To forge planning links across organizational divisions, e.g. R and D
and marketing
To evaluate plans against the chief executive's formulated strategy
To monitor the agreed plans

The planner is a coordinator who sees that the planning is done—not a formulator of goals and strategies. The planner's responsibility has three basic dimensions. They are:

1 Directive
2 Supportive
3 Administrative

In his *directive* role, the planning executive acts on behalf of top management to supervise the planning procedure to promote orderly and disciplined implementation of the planning process. This function can be performed well only when managers have both the *ability* and *willingness* to make it happen. The planning executive is likely to be more effective by acting in a *supportive* than in a *directive* role.

A *supportive* role brings the planning executive into service as an internal consultant and advisory resource. In this role he:

Advises line management on the application of planning principles
Assembles background information to provide insight into the economy, industries, markets, investment alternatives, etc., which are relevant to each business he serves
Directs or supports forecasting of the economy, industries and end-user markets
Renders assistance in installing progress-monitoring systems and interpreting their output
Renders assistance to line executives in applying advanced methods and procedures
Provides other internal and consulting assistance to line managers in preparing their plans and monitoring their progress

In their *administrative* role, planners ensure that planning procedures are implemented on schedule and that communications are accurate and rapid. In this role, it is suggested that they have limitations. They can provide coordinating and communicating services, but they cannot enforce them. If line management does not participate willingly, someone else with the appropriate authority must take corrective or disciplinary action.

Again, when this is taken in the context of the failures of marketing planning systems, it is clear that an understanding of the proper role of the Planning Department is an important determinant of planning success.

Marketing planning cycle

The schedule should call for work on the plan for the next year to begin early enough in the current year to permit adequate time for market research and analysis of key data and market trends. In addition, the plan should provide for the early development of a strategic plan that can be approved or altered in principle.

A key factor in determining the planning cycle is bound to be the degree to which it is practicable to extrapolate from sales and market data, but generally speaking successful planning companies start the planning cycle formally somewhere between nine and six months from the beginning of the next fiscal year.

It is not necessary to be constrained to work within the company's fiscal year; it is quite possible to have a separate marketing planning schedule if that is appropriate, and simply organize the aggregation of results at the time required by the corporate financial controller.

Planning horizons

It is clear that one- and five-year planning periods are by far the most common. Lead time for the initiation of major new product innovations, the length of time necessary to recover capital investment costs, the continuing availability of customers and raw materials, and the size and usefulness of existing plant and buildings, are the most frequently mentioned reasons for having a five-year planning horizon.

Many companies, however, do not give sufficient thought to what represents a sensible planning horizon for their particular circumstances. A five-year time span is clearly too long for some companies, particularly those with highly versatile machinery operating in volatile fashion-conscious markets. The effect of this is to rob strategic plans of reality. A five-year horizon is often chosen largely because of its universality. Secondly, some small subsidiaries in large conglomerates are often asked to produce strategic plans for seven, ten and sometimes fifteen years ahead, with the result that they tend to become meaningless exercises. While it obviously makes sense for, say, a glass manufacturer to produce twelve-year plans because of the very long lead time involved in laying down a new furnace, it does not make sense to impose the same planning time scale on small subsidiaries operating in totally different markets, even though they are in the same group. This places unnecessary burdens on operating management and tends to rob the whole strategic planning process of credibility.

The conclusion to be reached is that there is a natural point of focus into the future, beyond which it is pointless to look. This point of focus is a function of the relative size of a company. Small companies, because of their size and the way they are managed, tend to be comparatively flexible in the way in which they can react to environmental turbulence in the short term. Large companies, on the other hand, need a much longer lead time in which to make changes in direction. Consequently, they tend to need to look further into the future and to use formalized systems for this purpose so that managers throughout the organization have a common means of communication.

How the marketing planning process works

There is one other major aspect to be considered. It concerns the requisite location of the marketing planning activity in a company. The answer is simple to give. Marketing planning should take place as near to the marketplace as possible in the first instance but such plans should then be reviewed at high levels within an organization to see what issues have been overlooked.

It has been suggested that each manager in the organization should complete an audit and SWOT analysis on his own area of responsibility. The only way that this can work in practice is by means of a *hierarchy* of audits. The principle is simply demonstrated in Figure 12.4.

This illustrates the principle of auditing at different levels within an organization. The marketing audit format will be universally applicable. It is only the *detail* that varies from level to level and from company to company within the same group. For example, any one single company can specify without too much difficulty the precise headings under which information is being sought. In the case of an industrial lubricants company, under an assessment of the market environment, information and commentary was required on capital investment schemes, foreign investments, economic growth rates, health and safety regulations (clearly important in this market), inflation rates, tariff protection, etc., together with an assessment of their effect on the lubricants market.

Under the heading 'market', key product groups and key market sectors were defined (in this case the British Standard Industrial Classification System was used). It was left to each subsidiary to specify what the particular key industries were in their particular territories. Data sheets were provided for this purpose.

In the case of the competitive and the internal audit, each operating unit was merely asked to provide, for each major product, its strengths and weaknesses and those of competitive products; likewise for opportunities and threats. To assist with this process, a check list was provided which

Hierarchy of audits

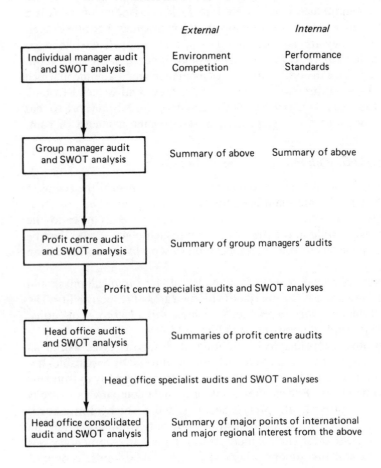

Figure 12.4

included, *inter alia*, international approvals from original equipment manu-facturers, compliance with health and safety regulations, and so on. Some data sheets were provided for market share analysis by key industry, pricing against competitive products, etc.

At each operating level, this kind of information can be gathered in by means of the hierarchy of audits illustrated in Figure 12.4 with each manager completing an audit for his area of accountability. While the overall format can be universal for a large and diversified group, uniformity is only necessary for units engaged in like activities. The advantages which accrue to the several headquarters levels are substantial in terms of measuring worldwide potential for products and market segments. Without such an information-collecting vehicle, it is difficult to formulate any overall strategic view.

It has to be recognized that information and data are not always readily available in some parts of the world, in the sort of format which is required, but given training, resources and understanding between headquarters and units, it is surprising how quickly information links can be forged which are of inestimable value to both sides. The same is also true of agents and distributors, who quickly respond to the give and take of such relationships in respect of audit-type information, which they inevitably find valuable for their own business.

Since in anything but the smallest of undiversified companies it is not possible for top management to set detailed objectives for operating units, it is suggested that at this stage in the planning process, strategic guidelines should be issued. One way of doing this is in the form of a *strategic planning letter*. Another is by means of a personal briefing by the chief executive at 'kick-off' meetings. As in the case of the audit, these guidelines would proceed from the broad to the specific, and would become more detailed as they progressed through the company towards operating units. Table 12.1 contains a list of the headings under which strategic guidelines could be set.

Under marketing, for example, at the highest level in a large group, top management may ask for particular attention to be paid to issues such as the technical impact of microprocessors on electromechanical component equipment, leadership and innovation strategies, vulnerability to attack from the flood of Japanese and European products, and so on. At operating company level, it is possible to be more explicit about target markets, product development, and the like.

It is important to remember that it is top management's responsibility to determine the strategic direction of the company, and to decide such issues as when businesses are to be milked, where to invest heavily in product development or market extension for longer term gains, and so on. If this is left to operating managers to decide for themselves, they will tend to opt for actions concerned principally with *today's* products and markets, because this is what they are judged on principally. There is also the problem of their inability to appreciate the larger, company-wide position.

Nevertheless, the process just described demonstrates very clearly that there is total interdependence between top management and the lowest level of operating management in the objective and strategy setting process. In a very large company without any procedures for managing this process, it is not difficult to see how control can be weakened and how vulnerability to rapid changes in the business environment around the world can be increased. This interdependence between the top-down/bottom-up process is

Table 12.1   Chief executive's strategic planning letter (possible areas for which objectives and strategies or strategic guidelines will be set)

Financial	*Operations*
Remittances	Land
— dividends	Buildings
— royalties	Plant
Gross margin %	Modifications
Operating profit	Maintenance
Return on capital employed	Systems
Debtors	Raw materials
Creditors	— supplies
Bank borrowings	— purchasing
Investments	Distribution
Capital expenditure	— stock and control
Cash flow controls	— transportation
	— warehousing
Manpower and organization	*Marketing*
Management	Target markets
Training	Market segments
Industrial relations	Brands
Organization	Volumes
Remuneration and pensions	Market shares
	Pricing
	Image
	Promotion
	Market research
	Quality control
	Customer service

illustrated in Figures 12.5 and 12.6, which show a similar hierarchy in respect of objective and strategy setting to that illustrated in respect of audits.

Having explained carefully the point about *requisite* marketing planning, these figures also illustrate the principles by which the marketing planning

Strategic and operational planning

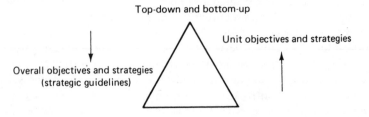

Figure 12.5

process should be implemented in any company, irrespective of whether it is a small exporting company or a major multinational. In essence, these exhibits show a *hierarchy* of audits, SWOT analyses, objectives, strategies and programmes.

Figure 12.7 is another way of illustrating the total corporate strategic and planning process. This time, however, a time element is added, and the relationship between strategic planning letters, long-term corporate plans and short-term operational plans is clarified. It is important to note that there are two 'open loop' points on this last diagram. These are the key times

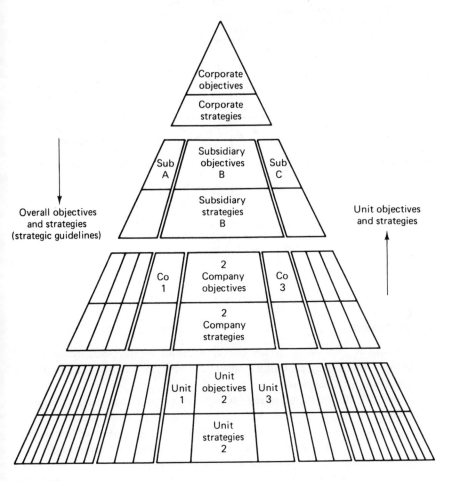

Strategic and operational planning

Figure 12.6

in the planning process when a subordinate's views and findings should be subjected to the closest examination by his superior. It is by taking these opportunities that marketing planning can be transformed into the critical and creative process it is supposed to be rather than the dull, repetitive ritual it so often turns out to be. These figures should be seen as one group of illustrations showing how the marketing planning process fits into the wider context of corporate planning.

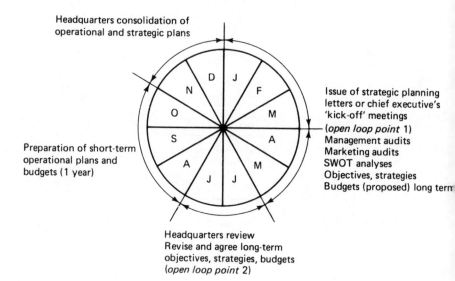

Figure 12.7

Final thought

In conclusion, we must stress that there can be no such thing as an off-the-peg marketing planning system, and anyone who offers one must be viewed with great suspicion.

In the end, marketing planning success comes from an endless willingness to learn and to adapt the system to our people and our own circumstances. It also comes from a deep understanding about the *nature* of marketing planning, which is something that in the final analysis cannot be taught.

Success comes from *experience*. Experience comes from making mistakes. We can minimize these if we combine *commonsense* and *sweet reasonable-*

ness with the *models* provided in this book. But be sure of *one* thing, above all else. By themselves, the models will not work. However, if you read this book carefully and use the models sensibly, marketing planning becomes one of the most powerful tools available to a business today.

We wish you every success in your endeavours.

Application questions

1 Does the principle of hierarchies of audits, SWOTs, objectives, strategies and programmes apply in your company? If not, describe how they are handled.
2 If it is, describe in what ways it differs from the principles outlined here.
3 Design a simple system for your company, or describe in what ways your existing system could be improved.

Glossary of Marketing Planning Terms

Assumptions The *major* assumptions on which the marketing plan is based.

Benefit A perceived or stated relationship between a product feature and the need the feature is designed to satisfy. *See also* Differential advantage *and* Feature.

Business plan A plan commonly intermediate between a company's strategic plan and its annual marketing plan. The purpose of the business plan is to establish the broad business objectives and strategies to be pursued by the business unit or centre over a time period of as many as five years. In this respect, business plans are similar to strategic plans which concern themselves with equally long time frames. Business plans are like strategic plans in one other respect: usually they deal with such strategic considerations as new product development, product acquisition, and new market development to achieve desired financial goals. Business plans also require extensive marketing input for their formulation and in this respect, they share characteristics in common with marketing plans. However, business plans generally do not include action programmes—a feature typical of marketing plans—but simply spell out intentions and directions. For example, if new product development was among the strategies to be pursued, this would be stated along with appropriate supporting rationale. However, the statement of this strategy would not be accompanied by a new product development plan.

Charter A statement of the chief function or responsibility of an operating unit within an organization made up of several operating units. *See also* Mission.

Core strategy   A term used in marketing to denote the predominant elements of the marketing mix, selected by marketing management to achieve the optimum match between the benefits customers seek and those the product offers. This process of selection is sometimes referred to as 'making the differential advantage operational.'

Differential advantage   A benefit or cluster of benefits offered to a sizeable group of customers which they value (and are willing to pay for) and which they cannot obtain elsewhere. *See also* Feature *and* Benefit.

Distribution   A term used in marketing to refer to the means by which a product or service is made physically available to customers. Distribution encompasses such activities as warehousing, transportation, inventory control, order processing, etc. Because distribution is the means of increasing a product's availability, it is also a tool which can be used by marketing management to improve the match between benefits sought by customers and those offered by the organization.

Experience effect   It is a proven fact that most value-added cost components of a product decline steadily with experience and can be reduced significantly as the scale of operation increases. In turn this cost (and therefore price advantage) is a significant factor in increasing the company's market share.

Feature   A characteristic or property of a product or service such as reliability, price, convenience, safety, and quality. These features may or may not satisfy customer needs. To the extent that they do, they can be translated into benefits. *See also* Benefit *and* Differential advantage.

Gap   In marketing terms, the difference between a product's present or projected performance and the level sought. Typically, the gaps in marketing management are those relating to return on investment, cash generation or use, return on sales, and market share.

Gap analysis   The process of determining gaps between a product's present or projected performance and the level of performance sought. *See also* Gap.

Growth/share matrix   A term synonymous with 'product portfolio' which in essence is a means of displaying graphically the amount of 'experience' or market share a product has and comparing this share with the rate of growth of the relevant market segment. With the matrix, a manager can decide, for example, whether he or she should invest in getting more 'experience'—that is, fight for bigger market share—or perhaps get out of the market altogether. These choices are among a number of strategic alternatives available to the manager—strategic in the sense that they not only affect marketing strategy but determine use of capital within the organization. *See also* Experience effect.

Marketing audit A situational analysis of the company's current marketing capability. *See also* Situational analysis.

Marketing mix The 'tools' or means available to an organization to improve the match between benefits sought by customers and those offered by the organization so as to obtain a differential advantage. Among these tools are product, price, promotion and distribution service. *See also* Differential advantage.

Marketing objectives A statement of the targets or goals to be pursued and achieved within the period covered in the marketing plan. Depending on the scope and orientation of the plan—whether, for example, the plan is designed primarily to spell out short-term marketing intentions or to identify broad business directions and needs—the objectives stated may encompass such important measures of business performance as profit, growth and market share.

Marketing objectives with respect to profit, market share, sales volume, market development or penetration and other broader considerations are sometimes referred to as 'primary' marketing objectives. More commonly, they are referred to as 'strategic' or 'business' objectives since they pertain to the operation of the business as a whole. In turn, objectives set for specific marketing sub-functions or activities are referred to as 'programme' objectives to distinguish them from the broader business or strategic objectives they are meant to serve.

Marketing plan Contains a mission statement, SWOT analysis, assumption, marketing objectives, marketing strategies and programmes. Note that the objectives, strategies and policies are established for each level of the business.

Market segment A group of actual or potential customers who can be expected to respond in approximately the same way to a given offer; a finer, more detailed breakdown of a market.

Market segmentation A critical aspect of marketing planning and one designed to convert product differences into a cost differential that can be maintained over the product's life cycle. *See also* Product life cycle.

Market share The percentage of the market represented by a firm's sales in relation to total sales. Some marketing theorists argue that the term is misleading since it suggests that the dimensions of the market are known and assumes that the size of the market is represented by the amount of goods sold in it. All that is known, these theorists point out and correctly, is the volume sold; in actuality, the market may be considerably larger.

Mission A definite task with which one is charged; the chief function of an institution or organization. In essence it is a vision of what the company is or is striving to become. The basic issue is: 'What is our business and what should it be?' In marketing planning, the mission statement is the starting point in the planning process, since it sets the broad parameters within which marketing objectives are established, strategies developed, and programmes implemented. Some companies, usually those with several operating units or divisions make a distinction between 'mission' and 'charter'. In these instances, the term 'mission' is used to denote the broader purpose of the organization as reflected in corporate policies or assigned by the senior management of the company; the term 'charter', in comparison, is used to denote the purpose or reason for being of individual units with prime responsibility for a specific functional or product-market area.

Objective A statement or description of a desired future result that cannot be predicted in advance but which is believed, by those setting the objective, to be achievable through their efforts within a given time period; a quantative target or goal to be achieved in the future through one's efforts, which can also be used to measure performance. To be of value, objectives should be specific in time and scope and attainable given the financial, technical and human resources available. According to this definition, general statements of hopes or desire are not true 'objectives'. *See also* Marketing objectives.

Planning The process of pre-determining a course or courses of action based on assumptions about future conditions or trends which can be imagined but not predicted with any certainty.

Policies Guidelines adopted in implementing the strategies selected. In essence, a policy is a summary statement of objectives and strategies.

Positioning The process of selecting, delineating and matching the segment of the market with which a product will be most compatible.

Product A term used in marketing to denote not only the product itself— its inherent properties and characteristics—but also service, availability, price, and other factors which may be as important in differentiating the product from those of competitors as the inherent characteristics of the product itself. *See also* Marketing mix.

Product life cycle   A term used in marketing to refer to the pattern of growth and decline in sales revenue of a product over time. This pattern is typically divided into stages: introduction, growth, maturity, saturation and decline. With time, competition among firms tends to reduce all products in the market to commodities—products which are only marginally differentiable from each other—with the result that pioneering companies—those first to enter the market—face the choice of becoming limited volume, high-priced, high-cost specialty producers or high-volume, low-cost producers of standard products.

Product portfolio   A theory about the alternative uses of capital by business organizations formulated originally by Bruce Henderson of the Boston Consulting Group, a leading firm in the area of corporate strategy consulting. This theory or approach to marketing strategy formulation has gained wide acceptance among managers of diversified companies, who were first attracted by the intuitively appealing notion that long-run corporate performance is more than the sum of the contributions of individual profit centres or product strategies. Other factors which account for the theory's appeal are: (1) its usefulness in developing specific marketing strategies designed to achieve a balanced mix of products that will produce maximum return from scarce cash and managerial resources; and (2), the fact that the theory employs a simple matrix representation useful in portraying and communicating a product's position in the market place. *See also* Growth/share matrix.

Programme   A term used in marketing planning to denote the steps or tasks to be undertaken by marketing, field sales and other functions within an organization to implement the chosen strategies and to accomplish the objectives set forth in the marketing plan. Typically, descriptions of programmes include a statement of objectives as well as a definition of the persons or units responsible and a schedule for completion of the steps or tasks for which the person or unit is responsible. *See also* Strategy statement *and* Marketing objectives.

Relative market share   A firm's share of the market relative to its largest competitor. *See also* Market share.

Resources   Broadly speaking, anyone or anything through which something is produced or accomplished; in marketing planning, a term used to denote the unique capabilities or skills that an organization brings to a market or business problem or opportunity.

Situational analysis The second step in the marketing planning process (the first being the definition of mission), and reviews the business environment at large (with particular attention to economic, market and competitive aspects) as well as the company's own internal operation. The purpose of the situational analysis is to identify marketing problems and opportunities, both those stemming from the organization's internal strengths and limitations, and those external to the organization and caused by changes in economic conditions and trends, competition, customer expectations, industry relations, government regulations and, increasingly, social perceptions and trends. The output of the full analysis is summarized in key-point form under the heading SWOT (strengths, weaknesses, opportunities and threats) analysis; this summary then becomes part of the marketing plan. The outcome of the situational analysis includes a set of assumptions about future conditions as well as an estimate or forecast of potential market demand during the period covered by the marketing plan. Based on these estimates and assumptions, marketing objectives are established and strategies and programme formulated.

Strategy statement A description of the broad course of action to be taken to achieve a specific marketing objective such as an increase in sales volume or a reduction in unit costs. The strategy statement is frequently referred to as the connecting link between marketing objectives and programmes—the actual concrete steps to be taken to achieve those objectives. *See also* Programme.

Target Something aimed at; a person or group of persons to be made the object of an action or actions intended, usually to bring about an effect or change in the person or group of persons, e.g. our target is the canned food segment of the market.

Index

212